Indian Ringne

Indian Ri

Indian Ringnecks (

by

Lindy Everbridge

Table of contents

Introduction

Among all the parrot species in the world, The Indian Ringneck is probably the most favorite among bird lovers as pets. These birds are known to be highly intelligent and extremely elegant. Whenever you think of a parrot, the first image that comes in your mind is a bright green colored bird which is the Indian Ringneck. That shows how common these species are and how popular they are as a species.

Native to Africa and Asia, these birds from the Psittacine family have been domesticated all over the world. They have been domesticated for several centuries now, so much so that they are believed to be meant for domestication only. Their ability to make wonderful companions and the ease with which they take to their human families has made them so popular.

Like any bird in this family, the Indian Ringneck is also extremely intelligent. This means that the bird can be trained to perform several tricks and can even be taught how to talk. Needless to say, these birds are also among the most entertaining of all parrots. Even watching them play by themselves in their cage can be highly relaxing and quite comical, too.

Indian Ringnecks are known to form strong bonds with their human families. They have the strongest bond with the primary caretaker but will also love their human "flock" dearly.

When you bring home an Indian Ringneck, you need to be sure that you can meet the physical and mental demands of these birds. When not taken good care of, these birds tend to develop several health issues as well as behavioral issues.

If you are planning to have a pet parrot at home, you need to remember that it is not enough to have a fancy cage with a bowl of seeds in it. You need to constantly work towards forging a good relationship with your bird to keep him happy and healthy.

There are several things that you need to think about when you bring a parrot home such as:

- Feeding
- Housing
- Creating a bond
- Training
- Correct introduction to the new environment
- Healthcare
- Safety precautions
- Breeding
- Financial commitment

There is a lot more that you will have to learn about these birds before you make a commitment. An Indian Ringneck can live up to 50 years of age. So, you need to be sure that you have all the resources available to take care of your bird for that time period.

This book tells you everything that you need to know in order to give your bird a happy and healthy life. The tips are based on discussions with other Ringneck owners. Therefore, they are practical and easy to apply when you bring your bird home. You must remember to always keep learning about the species of parrot that you bring home. The more you understand the natural behavior of the bird, the better you will be able to provide for him when you bring him home as a pet.

Chapter 1: Introduction to Indian Ringnecks

Leaning about the natural history and the captive history of a species can tell you a lot about the care that they need. This chapter takes you through all the details that you need to know about the Indian Ringneck so that you are not only able to identify the species but are also able to prepare for the bird as needed.

1. Identifying Indian Ringnecks

Each species of birds has certain physical characteristics that help you identify them. With the Indian Ringnecks, one of the most striking features is the coloration of their plumage. While the most common color associated with these birds is bright green, they have a range of colors that are bright or pastel depending on the hybrid and the sub-species. Indian Ringnecks have colors including lime green and yellow. Irrespective of the color of the feathers, the birds have a bright red band around the neck which gives them their name. They also have a very unique long tail that helps you identify them.

Indian Ringnecks are medium sized birds. They grow to a length between 36-43 cms from the head to the tip of the tail. The tail accounts for half the length of the body. The wings are usually about 7 inches long. These birds are also lighter than other species of parrots of the same size. They weight 115-140 grams on an average.

Indian Ringnecks have a characteristic hooked beak. This beak is usually bright red in color with a distict black tip. The lower bill has a tip that is paler and is mostly blackish in color. The feet are ash grey or greenish in color. These birds have a pale yellow iris which makes it look like they always have a sparkle in the eye.

In the wild these birds may have a bluish or yellowish tinge to their largely green plumage. These colors are found in the under plumage. It may also be lighter than the rest of the body.

A hint of blue may be seen in the nape of the neck, extending to the back of the bird's head. They have bright green tail feathers with a slight yellow tinge in the center sometimes. They have distinct strips of black feathering that runs down the chin area.

These birds are not sexually dimorphic. This means that the male and the female look very similar to one another. In mature males, however, there are some physical traits that are distinctive. For instance, they have a band on the neck that is red in color. This band goes up to the eyes from the beak. There is another band that goes to the neck, tapering down from the lower bill. This lower line then connects with the black ring that you see on the neck. In case of color mutations such as the blue parrot, the ring may be white in color.

In the case of females, this black line is not seen. They may not even have the black collar on the neck. In case the female has a black ring around the neck, the color is much paler in comparison to males.

It is difficult to tell these birds apart when they are younger. Techniques like DNA gender testing or surgical methods are recommended in these cases.

Juvenile birds resemble the adult female for the most part. The plumage, however, is a little paler. They do not have any black markings on the neck or the chin. They do not have a ring near the neck either. Mature males have a blue tint near the neck, which is not evident in the juveniles.

When the birds are over 2 years old, they develop the same plumage as an adult. In very rare cases, a red colored collar may appear on the neck of the juvenile bird even at the age of one.

2. Taxonomy

Also known as the rose ringed parakeet, this bird originates from areas around Africa and Asia. The bird belongs to the genus *Psittacula,* which is derived from the Latin word *psittacus,* which means parrot.

Scientifically, the Indian Ringneck is classified as *Psittacula krameri.* The scientific name commemorates Australian naturalist, Wilhelm Heinrich Kramer.

Research has revealed that Indian Ringnecks have DNA quite similar to the Mauritius parakeet. The resemblance is so much that it is often debated if the latter is, in fact, an African or Asian subspecies of the former.

There are four subspecies of the Indian Ringneck as of now. These fall into the categories of Asian and African Subspecies. The four subspecies are:

- **African Rose Ringed Parakeet:** These birds commonly inhabit the West African zone including Guinea, Senegal, East to West of Uganda, Southern Mauritiana, Egypt and the Southern parts of Sudan. You will see these birds flocking with other birds that belong to Giza and the Nile Valley. Small populations of the bird have been seen in the North Coast of Africa and in Sanai. Around the 1980s, these birds migrated and started to breed in Israel. In areas that birds migrate to breed, they are often called invasive species.
- **Abyssinian rose ringed parakeet:** Found along the northern Sennar region, the western coast of African, Ethopia, Northwester areas of Somalia and Sudan, these birds are another African subspecies.
- **Indian rose ringed parakeet:** This is a subspecies that is native to India. There are some populations that have migrated to various parts of the world. As a result, these birds are also found in Britain, Australia and the United States.
- **Boreal rose ringed parakeet:** These birds are commonly found in the northern region of India and in parts of Nepal, Bangladesh, Pakistan and Burma. Even these birds have migrated to different parts of the world and have formed successful feral populations.

Since these birds are found almost all over the world, it is clear that they have been part of human civilization for quite some time. These birds have been known to be domesticated even when the Roman Empire reigned.

They have been mentioned in the artwork and in the literature. One of the most interesting factors about this bird is that even though it is a tropical species, it has become popular across the world. The reason for this is their compatibility with human beings and their temperament.

3. Are the Asian and African species different?

Broadly, ringnecks are classified as the Asian and African species. Now, although these species are quite similar in their appearance, there are a few minor differences that are evident only to those who have some experience with these birds. One thing that they have in common is that both of them make wonderful pets.

Although these birds are very similar, knowing the minute differences is necessary when you decide to bring these birds home. The differences are as follows:

Color Differences

- At first glance, the two types of Ringnecks look exactly the same. However, the Asian species have plumes that are a more vibrant green shade. In the case of the African species, the outer feathering is lime green in color.
- African Ringnecks have a thicker black collar in the male birds. This collar is more prominent in the African species.
- In the Asian variety, the rose ring is more prominent and is much brighter in comparison to the African variety.
- African Ringnecks have a plum colored beak while the Asian Ringnecks have a bright red colored beak.

Size Differences

- One of the biggest differences between the African and Asian species is their size.
- African Ringneck parrots are similar to cockatiels in size and are much smaller than the Asian species. They grow to a size of about 11-13 inches from the head to the tip of the tail.
- The Asian species are much larger and are an average of 16 inches in length.

- Another distinguishing factor is the ratio of the tail to the body. The tail is longer in comparison to the body in the African Ringnecks. This ratio is higher in the African species in comparison to the Indian Ringnecks.
- Weight is also quite different for each species. The Asian varieties are heavier, usually growing up to 125 grams. On the other hand, the African varieties do not exceed 120 grams in weight.

Personality differences

- This is the most important thing for you to know if you are planning to bring home a ringneck. Indian Ringnecks are known to be more aggressive than the African Ringnecks. For those who are less experienced with parrots, the latter is recommended.
- For those who bring home an Asian Ringneck, it is necessary that they are more patient. You need to be more dominating towards the bird and will have to make sure that they are well trained.
- When they are younger, the Asian varieties tend to be nosier and more nippy.
- With both species, do not expect them to be too cuddly. While the African varieties are more tolerant, it is best to limit the petting to the side of the bird's neck. Any other touch is not appreciated by either species.

The difference between the two birds helps you decide which one you want to bring home. While it is not very different to have either species at home, the African species are easier to handle in comparison to the Asian species.

4. Captive History of Ringnecks

As mentioned before, Indian Ringnecks have been chosen as companions to people for centuries now. They have been mentioned several times in ancient literature and the folklore of India and Pakistan.

For several foreigners, this was type of parrot that they had never seen before. As a result, these birds were exported back to their respective countries from Pakistan and India. One of the most popular names associated with these birds is Alexander the Great. During his invasion in Asia, he was so fascinated by these birds that he got them exported to several areas near the Mediterranean region. It is believed that he was responsible for the large populations of these birds across the globe.

Today, these birds are a common pet in several countries such as Australia, US, South Africa and the United States.

These birds are native to Eastern and Central Africa, India and parts of Burma. The invaders of these regions and several monarchs are responsible for introducing these birds in Europe. When they visited these countries, the bird caught their fancy and they introduced them in their own countries.

Several mentions of these birds can be found in Ancient Greek literature. As early as 200BC, Archimedes mentioned these birds in his records. These birds have also been around in Great Britain for several centuries. The Royal Family also own a few birds.

Alfred Ezra, who was born in India, had several birds imported to Europe in the 1920s. He was fascinated by these birds even as a child. He was responsible for producing the first hybrid Lutino variety of these birds. However, the birds that he bred were not very healthy and did not live too long.

It was in the year 1932 that Duke of Bedford discovered methods to produce healthy Lutino varieties. As a result, he had several birds on his estate. It was his efforts that led to the popularization of these species.

Only around 1934, Alfred Ezra was successful in breeding healthy Lutinos. By this time, this variety was already being bred on several other bird farms.

Masauji Hachisuka produced a series of papers titled, "Variations among birds" in the year 1920. In these papers he mentions a man named MG Mallick who bred Indian Ringnecks in Calcutta. There are several stories and myths about these birds. One says that he owned two male birds who were kept in a cage that was made entirely of gold. It is also believed that he never bred these two birds with other species or even birds of the same species.

During the Second World War, the aviary of a British soldier residing in India produced the first ever blue Indian Ringneck. The parents were entirely green but they gave birth to an offspring that was blue in color.

Lutino Ringnecks had become quite popular across the globe around 1947. They were equal in number to the Indian Ringnecks, especially in countries like England.

It was not until 1949 that these birds were introduced in the USA. Sidney Porter is credited to have conducted a lot of research about the Lutino variety. He then obtained two Lutinos and two Indian Ringnecks in the year 1949. These birds were then bred in Fillmore California as an attempt to increase the Lutino population in the United States.

The Indian Ringneck had made its way into several countries by now and was considered a prized possession. Indians sold them to foreigners for large sums. Records show that a pair of blue Ringnecks were sold to breeders, Harold Rudkin and George West for a total sum of $1000 by a Calcutta based breeder in the year 1948. It is believed that these were the only two live birds in captivity.

To protect the wild populations of these birds and other exotic birds, the USA laid down several laws with respect to parrots. The bird would be allowed into the country only if the person bringing it had it for at least 30 days. Only then would the bird be considered a family pet.

However, Rudkin and West were unable to produce any evidence that they had these birds for the stipulated time period. As a result, they were returned to India.

In the same year, the two blues returned to India were purchased by the Duke of Bedford. He had them sent to David West in the year 1952. Following this, a successful breeding program was started to produce more blue Ringnecks.

Ray Thomas, one of the wealthiest aviculturists of his time, then had two turquoise Ringnecks imported from Calcutta. These birds were renamed as the Blue Simon. However, these birds were not the same blue as the Blue Indian Ringnecks. Therefore, he did not pay for the birds. He cared greatly for the birds and when he died, he passed them on the Dave West and Gordon Hayes who began breeding programs with this unique mutation.

By now, albino birds had also surfaced. In the year 1952, a Lutino variety was bred by the Duke of Bedford. Around the same time, the first albino was also created. However, the population of these birds could not be improved as there were very few Lutino male birds.

14 birds were raised in captivity by the year 1954 by Dave West and other breeders. Dave West had four birds and the others belonged to various breeders in England. The Duke of Bedford passed on his blue pair to the Keston Foreign Farm just before his death. Four more blue birds were bred through this pair.

A green and yellow harlequin was then found by a breeder named Edward Boosey from the Keston Foreign Farm. These birds were large and had beautiful yellow spots all over the body. They had yellow tail feathers and bright yellow flight feathers. However, these birds did not gain too much popularity immediately. The Keston Foreign Farm was also responsible for several albino birds.

Experiments with Indian Ringneck breeding are still being conducted across the globe. Several colorful varieties have been produced, making the bird an even more popular choice as a pet.

5. Habitat, Range and Distribution

Indian Ringneck parrots have a very vast native range. These birds are seen in most tropical regions of the world. Their range begins from the Western parts of Africa and stretches all the way to the Indian Subcontinent until the foothills of the Himalayas.

In Asia, the range of these birds includes Nepal, Pakistan and Southern parts of Vietnam. Of all the subspecies, the Indian Ringneck is most common. It is believed that these birds originated in Sri Lanka. Even in captivity, this is the most common sub-species of Ringnecks.

In Sri Lanka and India, these birds are seen mostly in forests and wooded areas. These birds are known to be extremely hardy and adaptable. As a result, they are also seen in areas that are mostly inhabited by human beings. Their habitat includes suburbs, agricultural areas and even farms. They are seen in places that are abundant in food sources and also nesting areas.

However, in most of their native ranges, the birds were considered as pests. As a result, they were trapped or even killed for damaging crop and targeting these crops for food.

Just like any other wild species of birds, the Indian Ringneck, too, only needs good food sources and nesting areas in order to thrive. The most preferred nesting sites for these birds is in the cavity of a tree. This is seen mostly in the rural and suburban areas of India.

In terms of food, these birds tend to eat a variety. Their diet includes flowers, seeds, nuts, grains, berries and fruits. As a result, their populations are able to thrive in such vast ranges. They are able to adapt the roosting requirements and their diet, depending on the region that they inhabit. One popular example is that of the Egyptian populations. These birds eat dates in summer and switch to mulberry in spring. They also choose palm trees for nesting. These birds derive food from the sunflower fields and the palm trees, too.

The populations in India, on the other hand, depend mostly on cereal grain as the food source during the warmer part of the year and on pigeon peas when it gets colder. These birds also travel long distances to obtain their food. They also love to forage. This makes them cause a lot of damage to orchards and farms, earning them the reputation of being pests.

These birds, as mentioned above, adapt very readily. Therefore, you can see their populations almost everywhere on the globe. There are thriving populations in Florida, California and Hawaii. You will also find these birds in the Middle East, Japan and Africa.

These tropical birds have found ways to adapt even to the harsh winters of Britain. As long as they have food sources, these birds will thrive just about anywhere.

This brings us to the feral populations of these birds across the globe.

6. Thriving across the globe

Because of their immense popularity as pets, Indian Ringnecks were exported to various countries. Some of these birds were released into the wild, where they thrived because of their amazing adaptability.

In most countries that these birds were released in, the number of predators were lower. They also had more food options because of people who fed them and also the gardens in these areas. These birds are able to get a constant supply of food that they prefer, including nuts, seeds, berries and fruits.

Now, Indian Ringnecks are known to inhabit the harsh, cold conditions on the foothills of the Himalayas. Of course, these birds would also be able to adapt to the conditions in parts of the world like Europe.

As a result, feral populations are not only found in the tropical regions but also in Europe. Some of these populations are also found in the United States.

There are several self-sustained flocks in parks in places like Tunis, Tripoli, Ankara and Tehran. Feral populations have even been recorded in Lebanon, UAE, Israel, Oman, Qatar and Bahrain. Some birds that escaped aviaries also thrived in parts of Australia.

It was around the mid-20th Century that these birds began to grow in numbers in Europe. Most of these populations are found in the south western suburbs of London.

In London, Indian Ringnecks are commonly found in Battersea Park, Crystal Palace Park, Richmond Park, Wimbeldon Common, Surrey, Hampstead Heath, Berkshire and Greenwich Park. Large populations of these birds, that have been renamed as the Kingston Parakeets are also found in the south-western parts of London. Thousands of birds belong to these feral populations.

Around the dawn of the millennium, about 6000 birds migrated to London from three major roosting areas. You can also find some populations in Essex, Margate, North East London, Ramsgate, Kent and Theydon Bois.

There are some smaller populations that have established themselves in places like Studland, Greenbank Park, Manchester, Dorset and Sefton Park. These birds have populations that surpass the native birds of Britain in size. It is also believed that rising populations of the Indian Ringnecks threatens the populations of the native birds. As a result, there have been some measures in order to reduce their population. However, these birds continue to grow in numbers in these regions.

The Netherlands is also home to some feral populations of the Indian Ringnecks. They are mostly found in the urban areas including Utrecht Rotterdam, The Hague and Amsterdam. Around 2010, the population of the birds grew from 10,000 to almost double the number seen as per the census in 2004.

Some birds were released in Brussels, Belgium, in the year 1974. These birds were released by the Attraction Park in Meli Zoo and Atomium. There are approximately 5000 Indian Ringnecks just in Brussels.

They have also been spotted in parts of Germany, mostly the Urban Areas including Weisbaden, Dusseldorf, North Hamburg, Cologne, Heidelberg, Bonn, Lugwidshafen and Rhine. There are a few hundred birds in each flock.

The most common areas inhabited by the birds in Europe include Rome, Paris and some areas in Palatine Hill Gardens. These birds can also be found in treetops in Trastevere, Janiculum, Villa Broghese, Orto Botanico de Palermo, Barcelona, Lisbon and Genoa.

Interactions with intraspecific birds in these regions have also given birth to several hybrids. These birds have bred with other subspecies of birds such as the Alexandrine Parakeet.

As the feral populations across the world increase, these birds are reducing in numbers in their native lands, especially South Asia. This is the result of the pet trade. Several laws have been passed to make sure that these birds are restored in number. Some birds have also been released into the wild from captivity deliberately. However, their populations have reduced over the years, specifically in India.

Some feral populations of these birds have also been recorded in Japan. In the 1960s, these birds were owned by several Japanese homes as pets. For this reason, they were imported in huge numbers. While some of the birds were released, others escaped captivity and began to form feral populations. Around the 1980s, large feral populations began to crop up in parts of Tokyo, Osaka, Nagoya, Niihata and Kyusu. Some of these birds diminished over time. However, research has revealed that a large number of these birds continue to thrive in the Tokyo Institute of Technology, Maebashi and even China city.

Wherever these birds have been introduced, they have had a significant impact on the natural biodiversity, the economy and the wellness of the areas.

7. Behavior and personality

For a long time, the Indian Ringneck has been considered a bird that is very nippy and aggressive. When they are young, these birds go through a "bluffing" phase. This is the reason for this reputation that the birds have. We will talk about this in detail in the following chapters. However, once they get over this phase, these birds are very friendly and actually make wonderful pets.

Indian Ringnecks are extremely intelligent birds, which makes them quite easy to tame. However, you need to make sure that you give them a lot of attention. If you restrict interactions to cleaning and feeding, the bird is likely to become detached. Even a bird who started out as friendly and loving can show changes in personality if neglected for a long time.

Hand feeding birds when they are younger is a great idea to make them tame. Birds that are handfed tend to be more trusting and comfortable around humans. As a result, the nippiness is also decreased. You must spend some time playing with your bird each day. You can even just take the bird out of the cage to pet him for a while. With Ringnecks, however, petting should be restricted to gently stroking the feathers. These birds are not very fond of being cuddled.

The high intelligence of these birds allows them to learn a lot of things by just observing the people in their environment. This is one of the reasons why these birds are so quick to pick up human vocabulary. They are known to learn close to 250 words, which is the highest in comparison to any other species of parrots. They can pick up most words by just hearing you say them often. For instance, words like hello or goodbye are among the first ones that your bird will pick up.

They do not have the quality of speech that can match a few other species, however. The more time you spend with your bird, the more words he will learn and the better his quality of speech will be. You can spend a lot of time with your bird if you can train him to sit on your shoulder. Even though they are not particularly fond of cuddles and hugs, these birds will never mind being on your arm or shoulder all day.

You have to ensure that the Indian Ringneck is mentally challenged everyday. This helps keep their mind active and also keeps them calm. If this is ignored, you can expect several behavioral issues. There are several toys created especially for this. You can also figure out foraging games or try to teach your bird new tricks to keep him engaged. Keeping him with you as you go about your routine is also a great way to stimulate his brain.

Forming a strong bond with your parrot is one of the most important things that you need to do. Studies have shown that female birds tend to develop stronger bonds in comparison to males. Of course, these birds also love being around their human flock. While they form a strong bond with one of the family members, usually the one who takes care of the bird, they are also quick to bond with your family.

You must make sure that your family also interacts with your bird. This is very important to prevent issues rising from jealousy. Indian Ringnecks can become possessive and will not appreciate the human that they have bonded with showing affection to anyone else. To prevent aggression stemming from jealousy, introduce your bird to more people and make sure that he is well socialized.

In the younger years, when the bird displays bluffing behavior, it is best to ignore it. Bad behavior is often a means to get your attention. You need to be dominant in a gentle way. This will help you have a better relationship with your bird. Positive reinforcement is also known to work with these birds. When your bird displays acceptable behavior, make sure you reward him.

Indian Ringnecks are very curious by nature. They love adventure. They also demand attention from their humans. They can become very vocal and talkative. They can talk continuously and can even be noisy at times. They tend to whistle, screech and make other sounds throughout the day.

For those who have not had a parrot before, understanding the behavior of these birds is a must before you make any sort of commitment. If you have a household with young children, they are not the ideal pets to have. They tend to get spooked quite easily, too. Ringnecks also have night frights quite often. They may screech and trash around if startled.

It is, no doubt, quite the challenge to bring an Indian Ringneck home. However, if you are ready to give them time and learn more about them, you can have a fantastic journey with these birds.

8. Ringneck myths

Considering that the Indian Ringneck has been part of human civilization for so many years, there are bound to be some myths and stories about the bird that have been going around. The trouble with these myths is that they often give the bird a bad reputation, making you think before you bring the bird home as a pet. Here are some myths that you should just shrug away if you do hear them:

They are terrible pets

You will hear this even from the experts and the breeders. As mentioned before, Indian Ringnecks go through a phase called bluffing when they are young. This is when they are very nippy. As a result, they have been tagged as aggressive bird.

However, bluffing is a passing phase that is, no doubt, difficult to deal with. If you are not prepared for this phase, you may begin to believe this myth as well. At this point the analogy of a difficult teenager serves us the best. Think about the way teens behave. They are moody and always seem to be angry.

When the Indian Ringneck is in this stage of development, they seem to behave in the same manner. However, with some patience and persistence, these extremely intelligent birds are quite easy to tame. You need to be slightly more dominant than the bird to help him overcome this phase.

You can leave them alone for a long time in the cage

Most owners tend to leave these birds alone assuming that they are aggressive. However, Indian Ringnecks are very social birds and need to bond with their flock to be healthy and happy. In the wild, these birds are always surrounded by their flock and will spend most of their time with their chosen mate.

It is true that these birds have been found alone at times. Unlike most parrots, Indian Ringnecks do not breed with the same mate all their lives. They look for a different mate each breeding season.

You need to give your Indian Ringneck ample attention in order to keep him mentally stimulated and happy. They are also happy when kept in aviaries with other birds. As long as the introductions are made correctly, they are quite peaceful and friendly.

Female Ringnecks do not talk as well as the males

Gender does not determine the number of words the birds pick up, training does. If you are able to spend enough time with your bird, you can teach them to speak well, irrespective of whether it is a male or a female.

It is possible that this rumor stems from the fact that male ringnecks are often chosen as pets over females. The reason for this is that males are more colorful and not because they have better talking abilities.

You can only tame Ringnecks when they are separated very early from the mother

Many people believe that only when hatchlings are taken out of the nest before opening the eyes will they become tame. This is not true. These birds are not aware of their environment for almost 10-15 days after their birth. If separated too early, they will not socialize as well as they possibly can.

In the wild, baby ringnecks receive a lot of attention from their parents. In fact, the mother will comfort the baby birds as they are being fed by the father. If you breed Ringnecks, you will have to make sure that you give the baby birds some cuddle time. If not, they tend to become noisy. Taming baby birds only depends on hand-feeding and the efforts that you take to socialize the bird and interact with him regularly.

Females tend to be more aggressive than males

This is another popular myth that makes female ringnecks less preferred as pets. In fact, it has been observed that females are easier to tame and even tend to be more loyal than male birds. They form very strong bonds with their family.

Female ringnecks love to spend time with you and are also more open to cuddling and petting. However, during the breeding season, females do get territorial.

This is the phase when the bird is hormonal and moody. If you are able to learn how to handle the bird and give her some privacy during the breeding season, you will not have any issues with her. In fact, territorial behavior during the breeding season is common with all species of parrots.

The behavior of the bird depends on the quality of color

There is no real source for this myth. However, the fact that males are preferred over females is often considered one of the reasons for this myth. Since males are more colorful, it was often assumed that if the bird is brightly colored, they behave well. As we have discussed already, it is only socialization that matters and not the color or the gender of the bird.

The Indian Ringneck is a fascinating bird. Now that you have enough information about the species, the next step is to understand the kind of care that they require. This is when you will be able to determine if you truly have the time and resources to bring one of these birds home.

Chapter 2: Being Prepared for Ringnecks

Preparation is key to having any pet. You need to ensure that your bird is comfortable in your home from the first day. It also takes a lot of work from your end to make sure that your bird is happy and safe. This chapter talks about everything that you need to do before you bring an Indian Ringneck into your home.

1. Legalities

Indian Ringnecks are popular pets, no doubt. However, with increased pet trade and threats to the native bird populations because of Ringnecks released from captivity, several countries have laid down strict laws with respect to owning these birds.

In India, especially, several states prohibit breeding or having these birds as pets. If you are thinking about bringing one of these birds home, the first thing you need to know is if you can legally have a Ringneck as a pet in the city that you are living in.

You can contact the local wildlife authority to learn about the license required to have an Indian Ringneck as a pet. The process of obtaining a license usually requires you to fill out a form with the concerned authority and submit a health certificate. Once you obtain a license, you will be able to keep your bird without any issues.

Even if the bird has not been banned in your city, here are some legal considerations with respect to these birds that you should be aware of.

- **The "No Pet" Clause:** Make sure you check your lease or rental agreement for a no pet clause. If your landlord does not permit you to have a bird in the premises, you could be evicted if caught with the bird. You can talk to your landlord and in some cases, they may allow you to have the bird with you in your home. In some parts of the world, there are some rights that you can exercise in case of the no pet clause:
  - If you have had the bird for over 6 months without any objection from the landlord, you may be allowed to continue to keep him or her.

- You need to be given a notice period before being evicted for breaching the "no pet" clause.

- **In case your bird bites someone:** If your parrot bites or injures another individual, they have the right to file a lawsuit against you. The lawsuit will be in your favor or against you depending upon the circumstances of the incident. For instance, if the victim was found provoking the bird by putting his hand into the cage or touching him without permission, the lawsuit is usually dropped. You will be held responsible, however, if your bird has a history of aggressive behavior. In that case, you may have to pay punitive damages and reimburse any medical bills.

- **Travel related legalities:** Almost all species of exotic birds, including Indian Ringnecks are protected by strict rules laid out by CITES. If you are planning to travel with your Indian Ringneck, you need to be sure that you are aware of all these legalities.

First, when you decide to take your bird to another country or state, you will have to check for a permit requirement. Some states will require a permit under the regulations of CITES while others will require you to take a local permit as well. For example, in the United States, you need a CITES permit as well as a Permit from the Endangered species act. Check for regulations of the wildlife department in your state, country and the country you are travelling to to be safe.

You will most likely need a permit form the country you are travelling from and from the country you are travelling to.

Your veterinarian is a reliable source of information. He will be able to help you obtain these permits as well. You can check the official CITES website and the websites of the wildlife departments of the countries involved.

- Plan your travels well in advance because most permits take two months at least for processing. If you have to make a business trip urgently, you will most probably have to make alternate arrangements for your Indian Ringneck.

- Here are a few things you need to have when you are planning a trip with your bird:

  - Proof that your bird was legally obtained. A breeder's health certificate is usually accepted.

  - The permit from the respective countries that you are going to travel to and from.

  - Completed declaration forms as required in the destination port.

  - A health certificate from your vet that is not more than 30 days old.

- Take a few copies of your permits just to be sure. You also need to be prepared to be questioned by authorities at both ports to confirm the reason for import or export of the bird. With all the documents in place, you will not have to worry about your bird too much. Just make sure that his wings are clipped to ease the process of customs.

- **Moving to another state**
  Make sure you learn the laws of each state pertaining to birds. In case you are caught with an Indian Ringneck, you can be fined, the bird may be confiscated and, in worst cases, the bird can also be euthanized. In some states, you can own the birds but you cannot sell or breed them. They are prohibited in some states as they can be a threat to the native population of birds and are also considered agricultural pests.

  You can bring the bird to some states, even if they are prohibited, for a period of not more than 48 hours. This is when they are in transit and have to pass by a certain state when you are travelling. For all the laws related to a state, contact their agricultural department or the wildlife authorities.

- **Burial laws**

  In most states, it is prohibited to bury pets within the city limits. This is mainly to prevent any contamination of their water systems or to prevent disease outbreak. It is best to bury your bird in a pet cemetery. Most cities have a dedicated pet cemetery that you can contact.

- **How many birds can you keep**

  There are zoning laws in some parts of the world. This means that there is a restriction on the number of pets you can have, irrespective of the species. Zoning laws are especially important when you plan to breed your Indian Ringnecks. You need to be sure of the size of the aviary and the number of birds that you can own as per the law. There can also be regulations set by your housing associations that restrict the number to 5 birds or pets per home.

- **Medical malpractice laws**

  There are certain laws that you can look into in case you are certain that your vet has caused injury or is responsible for the death of your bird. As per the law, every pet is considered your personal property. Therefore some courts will grant you complete reimbursement of any expenses that you may have incurred because of irresponsible medical practices by the law. If your bird is insured, then your insurance company may cover it as well.

- **Divorce laws with respect to birds**

  Since pets are considered personal property, they will come under claims when you are dividing your assets in case you get divorced. If you are unable to come to a mutual decision on who will get the bird, this matter is taken up by the court. In that case, the person who the bird has bonded with the most is usually given custody of the bird. The other person will receive the fair market value of the bird and may even get a reimbursement of any expenses that he or she has incurred when the bird was under their care.

2. Housing

Indian Ringnecks are considerably large birds and will have specific requirements in terms of housing. A well-fed and happy bird is extremely active and you want to make sure that the cage allows the bird to move around freely without any chance of injuries. When you are buying a cage for your bird, there are some simple tips that will come handy:

- The size of the bird should be such that the walls are at least 5-6 inches more than the bird's wingspan, vertically and horizontally.
- If you have multiple birds, you need to make sure that they can both spread their wings without touching each other or the walls of the cage.
- The bars should be close enough to ensure that your bird's head does not fit through it. If they are wide enough for you to put your fingers or a stick through, it should be good enough. That is actually quite necessary for training. In case of an Indian Ringneck, this should not be more than ¾ inch.
- Each individual bar should not be too thick. The bird should be able to hold it with its beak and climb.
- The cage should be made of stainless steel, preferably. Make sure that it does not have any traces of lead or zinc. Powder coated cages work well too.

For an Indian Ringneck the minimum dimensions of a cage are 36"X24"X48". The bigger it is, the better for your bird. It is never a good idea to have a suspended cage for any bird. They like to have a sense of security. So, placing the cage against the wall is ideal for them.

Make sure that your bird cage is away from the kitchen to prevent any toxic cooking fumes from harming your bird. You also need to make sure that your bird does not experience any drafts in the cage. So, the air conditioner vent should be way from it. Room temperature works best for all parrots.

Adding a swing or a sleeping tent in the cage is a great idea. This will give the bird a safe place for the bird to sleep in. You will get one in any local pet store. You could alternatively use a towel to cover one edge of the cage so that the bird is protected from any light or disturbance while sleeping.

Feeding Bowls: For an Indian Ringneck, you will need to have three clean bowls. One will be used for water, one for pellets and one for the natural or fresh food. These bowls must be placed in an area of easy access so that you can change the food and clean them every day. Make sure that the perch is not too close to the food bowl in height. Birds usually throw their head back after taking some water into their beaks. If they keep hitting themselves on the perch, they may stop drinking from the bowl. This is a huge problem which may eventually lead to issues such as dehydration and indigestion.

The substrate: The best substrate is newspaper. However, the newsprint that is available these days may have a lot of chemicals that are toxic for the birds. So, you will benefit a lot by getting a cage that has a grate on the floor so that the bird does not get too close to the substrate. You must never use anything with a rough texture such as sandpaper. This will damage your bird's feet severely. Wood shavings and chips are also not recommended for parrots and parakeets.

Maintaining the cage: The cage of your Indian Ringneck should be cleaned on a daily basis. You must remove all the droppings and any food that is spoiling out of the cage every day. Perches must be wiped clean every day to prevent any infection or health issues for your bird. Make sure that you also wash the bowls every day. If you find any toy that has droppings on it, wash it too.

If you are using a metal cage, you need to check for any rust or chipped paint. This holds true even for a stainless steel cage. You need to be on guard every time. These things can be toxic for your bird.

You can use soap and water to wipe down the cage. Just water will do as well. Make sure that the soap is very mild. You must wash the cage thoroughly with this mild solution and then top it off with a disinfecting wash using a solution of vinegar or bleach. If you are using vinegar, mix one part with 8 parts of water. If you are using bleach, one part will be mixed with 32 parts of water. Remember, you must always use any one of the above. If vinegar and bleaching powder mix accidentally, the solution that is created is toxic for your bird.

Use the same solutions to clean your bird's toys and perches once every 15 days. You must rinse this solution off thoroughly before you introduce your bird into the cage.

Your Indian Ringneck requires a clean and dry environment to thrive in. If you are not particular about the hygiene of the cage, the bird may develop various health issues related to unsanitary conditions. This may include mild infections or may cause serious diseases that may even be fatal at times.

3. Safety Measures

A human home is seldom bird friendly. Our homes consist of glass items, Teflon coated pans and of course AC vents that seem normal and mundane to us. These simple household items can be hazardous to your bird and it is necessary for you to take the following measures to bird proof your home:

- Avoid using Teflon coated pans. These pans release certain fumes that can be fatal for an Indian Ringneck or any other bird for that matter. If you cannot eliminate Teflon pans, you need to at least ensure that the housing area of the bird is away from the kitchen.

- Breakable items should be kept out of the flight path of your bird. It is best to avoid them altogether as they may cause serious accidents that you will most certainly regret. You can keep these delicate items in areas of the house that the bird will most likely not access.

- Lead weights on curtains and blinds should be removed as lead poisoning occurs quite easily when the bird comes in contact with it.

- Keep loose wires out of the way. Birds tend to tug at any loose wire and may get electrocuted in the process.

- Install a door to the kitchen. The kitchen has several hot items like pans, stove tops etc. that can cause serious burns to your bird if he sits on them unknowingly. If not, you can get special covers for these surfaces quite easily.

- Ceiling fans should be kept off whenever the bird is out of the cage. You must also avoid switching on table fans when the bird is flying around the house.

- Never keep plain glass windows spotlessly clean. Mark them by placing items like pots at the windowsill. You can even add stickers to these clean glass surfaces to ensure that the birds do not fly right into them and suffer from injuries.

- The cage should be kept away from hard surfaces. If you have a baby bird, he may attempt to fly and fall several times in the process. A fall on a hard cement floor can be fatal to the bird.

- Keep the cage away from the air conditioner or the radiator. Cold or hot emissions from these machines can cause several health problems in Indian Ringnecks. Keep the cage in an area of the house that is extremely cozy.

Once you have a bird in your home, you will always have to make sure that the doors and windows are shut. Whenever you put the bird back in the cage, lock the door properly. Also be careful when you open and close the door. If your bird is let out loose most of the time, slamming the door can lead to a trapped bird with multiple injuries. Lastly, be prepared to make changes as per the personality of your bird. All you need to remember is that any health risk should be out of the way entirely.

4. Questions to ask yourself

There are some questions you need to ask yourself before you bring the bird home. Having an Indian Ringneck is a big responsibility. Even with all the information about the species and learning everything about the bird, most new owners leave out some practical details that can pose several issues in the future. Here are some questions that you need to ask yourself before you bring the bird home.

Will you be able to give the bird enough time?

Most people opt for parrots as pets because they believe that these birds do not have to be walked or entertained like dogs or cats. However, they are anything but low maintenance. Your bird will demand a lot of attention and quality time. With Indian Ringnecks, it is important that the whole family has some time to spare for the bird in order to forge a good bond with him. Only when you are certain that you can spend that much time should you bring one of these birds home.

Can you afford the Indian Ringneck?

These birds cost between $150-$800 or £70-£500. This depends on the source you obtain your bird from. You also need to invest in other things that the bird requires such as the housing area, which will cost you approximately $100-$500 or £60-£200. Besides this you have other expenses such as veterinary costs, bedding, food, toys and more. Having an Indian Ringneck at home will cost you close to $500 or about £300 per year after you have made all the initial investments. If your bird develops a serious health condition, then your budget can really overshoot. Unless you are prepared to deal with these financial responsibilities, do not bring a bird home.

Can you handle the mess?

Parrots in general are messy birds. They will regurgitate food, throw the food around and paint the walls with sticky food bits, leave feathers and feather dander everywhere and of course, poop around the clock. Your bird may also have some accidents when he is let out of the cage. For people who cannot handle mess around the house, these birds can be very frustrating to have. If you are willing to clean up after the bird and be patient with him, then you can open your home to one. Did I mention that they can damage upholstery and even chew things once in a while?

Are you buying the bird as a gift?

A pet as a gift is a great idea, but for someone who can handle the responsibility. If you are gifting your bird to someone, make sure that you are aware of their schedule and their lifestyle before you do so. Getting carried away and gifting a parrot can lead to several issues. The biggest one is the chance of the bird being abandoned because the person is unable to handle the responsibility. In addition to that, if the bird does not receive the care that he needs, he could even develop serious behavioral issues that can lead to injuries to the person and his family.

Even when you are certain that a person has the necessary resources for an Indian Ringneck, arrange for meetings with the bird and behavior training sessions. Most often, people are not aware of the specific requirements of a particular species of bird.

Is the bird meant to be a gift for a child?

If you are thinking of getting the bird for your child in order to teach them how to care for a pet and be responsible, then stop right there. In fact, even pet stores and breeders do not sell Indian Ringnecks to children because they can be dangerous. The bluffing period, when the bird is young, can be especially dangerous. Children can get nipped at times and the strong beak of the bird can cause some serious damage.

Even though children are excited at first, they may lose interest over time. That means, you need to take over the reins and care for the bird. These birds live really long and need to be cared for properly in order for them to be healthy and for them to be at their best behavior.

Are you adding the Indian Ringneck to your aviary?

If you already have pet birds or want a companion for your bird, you can bring an Indian Ringneck home. However, you need to take care of quarantining and ensure that the birds are introduced correctly. Also, having two birds means twice the attention. If you are bringing an Indian Ringneck home as a companion for your other bird, it does not mean that they will not demand as much attention. In fact, if the bond between the birds becomes stronger than their bond with you, they may view you as an intruder and become extremely possessive of one another. This also leads to aggressive behavior such as nipping.

Can you provide the variety in diet that the bird needs?

It is not enough to fill the food bowls with birdseed everyday. Not having the right nutrition can lead to serious health issues for the bird. You need to be able to spend time to chop up fresh fruits and vegetables, make pellet mixes at home or prepare sprouts for your bird to give him the variety in diet that he needs. This also needs some time from your side on a daily basis.

Do you know that they have a long life span?

Once you bring an Indian Ringneck home, it is a responsibility for at least 30 years. In some cases, 50 years. Will you be able to keep them for so long? Sometimes these birds are handed down over generations. You need to really think ahead of you and also make plans for your own life well in advance. Will you have to move homes? What happens when you start a family? When you are unable to plan ahead, the result is that the birds often get abandoned.

The biggest cause for abandonment with respect to parrots is the fact that their owners did not plan ahead and did not expect it to be so much work. Birds with a history of abandonment develop serious behavior issues. You see, they form a bond that is very strong and are usually unable to cope with the loss of their home and their companion. This also makes it harder for them to find a new home. So, before you bring a parrot home, learn as much as you can and then make the decision.

5. Learn some bird vocabulary

There are some words related to birds that you need to learn as a parrot owner. This will make communication easier with your vet or breeder when you call them with doubts or questions about your bird. Here are some terms that you must know:

- **Cloaca:** Sometimes called the vent, this is the part of the bird that opens into the reproductive system, the digestive system and the urinary tract of the bird. Basically, this is where your bird poops from. The cloaca indicates good or poor health. If it looks dirty with dried poop and feathers stuck to it, it is a sign of poor health. This area is often the first indicator of poor health.

- **Preen Gland:** Also known as the Uropygial gland, this is a gland that is placed at the base of a bird's tail. It is the oil gland that produces a certain type of oil that keeps the bird's feathers intact. You will see your bird preening its feathers. It looks like he is trying to rub something on his feathers. The secretions of the preen gland are rubbed on the wings, feet and legs using the beak. This makes sure that the legs and feet are healthy. It also preserves the structure of the feathers. If your bird's preen gland is not functioning properly, you will notice dry and scaly legs and messy feathers. This is an immediate indication of poor health.

- **Choanal papillae**: You will notice many tiny projections near the cloaca of the bird. At all times, these projections or the choanal pappilae should be sharp and straight. If they are blunt or absent, it means that your bird is suffering from some sort of nutritional deficiency or respiratory issues.

- **Boing:** This is a fun toy that is curved to look like a spiral shaped rope. Birds love to pull and tug on these.

- **Blood feather**: When a new feather is emerging after molting, it has a rich supply of both arterial blood and venous blood. These feathers look thick and almost purple in color. When this feather becomes mature, the supply of blood recedes automatically.

- **Calcium to Phosphorus ratio:** Calcium and phosphorus form an important part of your bird's diet. You need to make sure that the ration is maintained at 1.5:1 to keep your parrot healthy and well nourished. This ratio is especially important for the females to help proper egg shell formation. In both the birds, this ratio also affects their neurological health.

- **Fledgling:** A baby bird that has been removed from the nest but is still unable to fly is called a fledgling. These birds are unable to eat on their own with the help of their parents or without being hand fed.

- **Weaning:** The process of shifting the bird from dependent feeding to eating solid food on its own is called weaning. This is when you can introduce proper adult food to the birds.

As you learn to take care of your bird and spend more time together, you will learn several other terminologies. If you don't understand something, ask your vet or breeder. You can even keep reading medical journals about pet health to learn more about your bird's anatomy.

Chapter 3: Sourcing an Indian Ringneck

There are three primary options when it comes to bringing an Indian Ringneck home. You can buy the bird from a breeder, choose a bird from a pet store or adopt one. Each source has its set of pros and cons that you need to be aware of before you buy your bird.

The most important thing is to ensure that the bird you bring home is healthy. If not, they can develop serious health issues within hours of being in your home. Of course, the health of the bird is even more important if you already have other pet birds in your home. Treating a sick bird can be very expensive. In addition to that, it is heart breaking to see them suffer from common illnesses that affect parrots.

1. Breeder or Pet Store?

These are the two most common sources to obtain your Indian Ringneck from. You may choose either one based on the convenience or based on recommendations that you get from other Indian Ringneck owners. What you need to remember is to ask the right questions and be sure that the birds are indeed healthy and bred in ethical conditions.

Buying from a breeder

There are two types of breeders; commercial breeders and backyard breeders. Commercial breeders are not recommended simply because they may not be practicing ethical breeding. These breeders are only interested in making money and will put the birds through a lot of stress. This leads to offspring that are unhealthy and sometimes poorly behaved. The backyard breeders on the other hand are interested in breeding these birds purely for passion's sake. They will usually specialize in one type of Indian Ringneck. However, they will have more humane and healthy conditions for the birds to grow up in.

Buying from a pet store

This is, definitely, the most convenient option. There will be several local pet shops that sell exotic birds and reptiles. These stores are ideal for you to find a healthy Indian Ringneck. You will possibly find various hybrids as well. You need to make sure that you talk to the pet store owner in detail about the health of the birds and also the amount of interaction these birds have had with people. That will help you understand the personality of the bird to some extent before you actually bring him into your home.

Questions you should ask

Whether you are buying from a breeder or from a pet store, you need to make sure that you ask all the right questions to ensure that you are bringing a good quality bird home. That will ensure that the bird stays healthy and happy in your home. Here are a few questions that you should ask:

How healthy is the bird?

It is a given that the breeder or the pet store will assure you that the bird is of top quality. But, you need to ask for other details related to the health of the bird. Ask if the bird has ever been taken to a vet. You need to know if the bird exhibited any health issues in the past. You also need to ask about any possible medicines that were given to the bird including the ones that are regularly placed in the formula give to hand raised chicks.

How much time has a bird spent with its actual parents?

This is to understand whether your bird has been hand raised or not. Usually, birds that have been hand raised are easier to train. This is a common notion simply because the bird is already imprinted with humans. There are several critical details such as how young was the bird when it was pulled out from the nest box. These early experiences are important in shaping the personality of your bird.

Was fledging done properly?

Flight is an important skill for birds. When they are raised in an aviary, fledging is very important. This means that the keepers should have given the bird enough time to learn the necessary flying skills before pulling it out of the nest. This makes sure that the musculature of the bird is of good quality. One important thing to ask is whether the bird is able to fly when it is wet. That shows if the wings are strong enough or not.

Was weaning done properly?

Weaning refers to cutting down on the baby formula or the feed from the parents. Sometimes these birds are forced to wean by just reducing the number of feeds in a day. You need to know if the bird had any particular favorites when it was being weaned. Also, if the baby bird rejected the syringe or the spoon, it is an indication of some form of stress or poor eating practices.

Does the bird have a plucking problem?

You need to ask if the bird has been plucked by the parents or other siblings. Even if the parents of the Indian Ringneck that you have chosen had problems related to plucking, you need to be cautious. This gives you a history of any possible feather grooming issue with your bird.

Have the birds been socialized?

Socialization is one of the most important things when it comes to your new bird. If the bird has been raised in such a way that it has not interacted with too many people or even other birds, there could be housebreaking issues. Has the bird seen other birds larger or smaller than itself? This is a very important question to ask if you are bringing a bird home into a multiple bird family.

What foods is the bird used to eating?

Some breeders and pet store owners raise the birds entirely on a seed based diet. This is unhealthy for your bird. This could mean problems related to nutrition, especially for Indian Ringnecks. Ask if the bird has eaten pellets and nuts. Has it ever been given fresh produce such as fruits and vegetables? If yes, what are the fruits that have already been offered to the bird?

Does the Indian Ringneck have any other outdoor experiences?

In this case, outdoor refers to his immediate surroundings. Has the bird been exposed to changes in seasons such as sunshine and rain or snow? How does he react to lightning and thunder? You also need to ask if the bird is comfortable with sounds like automobile noises, garage sounds and other loud sounds. You also need to know what kinds of toys the bird like and dislikes. There are several important experiences like music, sounds of electrical appliances etc that make the birds more familiar with our world. These birds are the easiest to acclimatize. If the bird has been exposed to these experiences, there are chances that he is already tame and easier to handle. Of course, you can discipline birds that have not been exposed these "human" experiences. If the birds have been overprotected, there are chances that they will turn out to be very unworldly and lethargic.

Has the bird had any traumatic experiences?

When the bird was pulled out from the nestbox, how did he react? Was there any physical or mental trauma or shock that the bird experienced at that time? You can even check the feathers of the bird to check for stress. If there are any black lines, there are chances of some sort of trauma. These lines are called stress lines. There are several other traumatic experiences that birds may experience. This includes flying into a window, a bad visit to the vet, any attack by a dog, cat or other bird or even an uncomfortable shipping container. You can even ask how the bird reacts to hats and moustaches. These are important questions with respect to Indian Ringnecks because they tend to pay a lot of attention to the smallest details.

Basically, when you are planning to bring an Indian Ringneck home, you need to check the history of the bird as thoroughly as you can. That will help you prepare your home accordingly. The bird that you have chosen could be extremely sensitive to certain things that you can just avoid in the first few weeks of your bird's stay in your home. That way he will be able to get more comfortable in your home and focus on adjusting to the new environment instead of dealing with fears.

As far as the health of your bird goes, ask all the questions that come to your mind. Even if you feel like you are being too difficult, it is alright. Bringing home an unhealthy bird is a lot of responsibility. In addition to that, you may find yourself heartbroken if the bird does not thrive well under your care. To be certain that your breeder or the pet store that you chose is credible, talk to a few clients of theirs. A reliable breeder or pet store will help you connect with their clients and discuss their experience. If they are hesitant to make this happen, you may begin to look for other options.

What are the return policies?

Some breeders and pet stores can also have online stores. Although it is recommended that you buy from someone whom you can visit at least once, some people may choose an online purchase because of the convenience or because of the availability of a particular breed. When you choose to have a bird shipped, check for the return policies. The bird may develop infections or health issues due to stress when they are shipped. If these problems are severe, you should be able to return the bird to the breeder. They usually have very strict policies when it comes to shipping the birds. In case returning or exchanging is not an option, you may want to look elsewhere.

Is buying online an option?

Many pet owners believe that buying from an online breeder is actually quite a good idea. It certainly is if the breeder is well known and has a reputation for selling only healthy birds. However, with a bird as expensive as the Indian Ringneck, this is not a risk that is worth taking.

Now, you need to understand that with online breeders, you have no way of knowing how the birds have been maintained. There could be several pictures on their website. However, unless you can check the place yourself or can have a friend or family member do that for you, it is advisable not to invest in online purchases.

There is a 50% chance that you will get a beautiful, healthy bird. However the other 50% is a risk that you cannot take with Indian Ringnecks. Even if you pay half the price of the bird as an advance, it is a good amount of money.

With online breeders, even a reputable one is not advisable for birds like this. You see, after the bird has been shipped, there is not much control that the breeder has over the travelling conditions of the bird.

There are chances that you will get a fatigued bird whose health has been compromised due to lack of food or proper transport conditions.

If you insist on online purchase of an Indian Ringneck for convenience purposes, here are a few things that you need to keep in mind:

- Only opt for breeders who can be recommended by friends and family. They should have personally made a purchase for the recommendation to be of value to you.

- Do not choose a breeder who is too far away from your city. It is best to choose someone in a city that you can reach in under 5 hours by flight. If your birds need to spend long hours on the flight, it is not good for his health.
- Ask for a health certificate with your bird. Tests should be based on blood and fecal samples. That helps you ensure that there are no chances of psittacosis in your Indian Ringneck.
- Ask your breeders to provide you with contacts of people that he has shipped birds to in the past. Any good breeder will share this information easily.

Of course, with online purchases, scams cannot be neglected. There are several individuals who will try to make a quick buck out of your requirement. Now, when you are looking online, you are going to look in a search engine most probably. This notifies people who run fake websites.

There have been instances when potential owners have received pictures of birds that belong to someone else. In these pictures, you will even see the owner of the bird that these scam websites claim to be themselves.

You can catch a scam pretty easily. They will approach you persistently to make a sale. In addition to that, they will ask you to pay small amounts in intervals. They will keep on adding new expenses like insurance, transport etc. An authorized breeder will know what all expenses are involved and will give you a full invoice and costing for transporting the bird.

When a breeder approaches you to make a sale, make sure you ask them questions about Indian Ringnecks. Ask them about the breeding season of the bird, the diet, the care required etc. These questions should be asked over the phone to make sure that they are not looking for answers online.

Anyone interested in just scamming you will have no idea about these birds most often.

Lastly, you need to ask them for contacts of people that they have already sold birds to. If they are reluctant or do not share this information for any other reason, you need to become aware that they are trying to scam you.

People have lost hundreds of dollars trying to make online purchases. Most of these websites will be pulled down within days of "making a sale" or getting an advance from people. Remember, never pay the full amount to a breeder until you receive the bird in good condition when you are placing an order online.

How do you know if the source is right?

There are some ideal conditions that have been mentioned above. But, these are not standards that help you decide if one breeder or pet store is better than the other or not. You must be open to different breeding practices, provided that they are ethical.

The only thing that you need to be sure of is that you are dealing with the right people who will take good care of your bird. Usually, breeders will allow you to take a bird home only when it is at least 3 months old. Now, this means that your bird is going to be under constant care of the breeder for this period. So if you are comfortable with the environment that your breeder is providing for the bird and if you feel a connection with the breeder or the pet store, you can definitely opt for them. Here are some standards that will help you decide if the breeder is good or not. Think of this as the first impression:

Are the cages clean?

If you notice that the cage is very messy with bird poop all over the place, it means that the breeder or pet store is not providing sanitary conditions for the bird to thrive in. The water bowl should be clean and free from feathers or excreta. If there are feathers stuck to the floor or the bars of the cage, it means that the bird has not been taken care of very well.

Do the birds have food and water?

The food bowl and the water bowl of the birds must be full and clean. This shows that the birds have abundant food available for themselves. You need to be sure that your bird has been fed well. This ensures that there are no nutrition related issues with your Indian Ringneck. It also shows an ethical and healthy environment for the birds. Parrots develop several behavioral issues when they are not taken care of. Lack of food, water and sanitation is a sign of neglect.

Are the birds healthy?

Indian Ringnecks are usually active birds that love to play. If you see that the bird is just sitting on the perch for a long time and shows no interest when you approach the cage, it is a sign of health issues. If you see too many feathers on the floor of the cage, it could mean that the bird is plucking (unless it is molting season). The eyes of Indian Ringnecks are usually bright and lively, the beaks are sharp and smooth, the feet are clean and free of lumps and the feathers are smooth and fur like. If you notice any abnormality in these characteristics of your bird, it is an indication of poor health. Make sure you speak to the breeder or the pet store owner about this.

Some breeders follow a closed aviary method. This means that they will not introduce new birds into their aviary easily. Even if they do, the birds are properly quarantined. This is a very good sign as the birds are kept free from any form of infection. Ask your breeder or pet store if they practice this method. These are some of the best people to make your purchase from.

Why are hand raised birds better?

If you are a first time buyer, insist on birds that have been handfed only. While it is possible to train Indian Ringnecks pretty easily considering their intelligence, it is not really a good idea to train the birds after you have brought them into your home if you are a first time owner.

Now, our fingers and hands are pretty intimidating to birds. They also closely resemble branches of the trees or even the worms to most birds. They are likely to take a bite on them or just nibble on your fingers as an attempt to find a suitable perch. With smaller birds, this is acceptable. But if you bring home a juvenile or adult Indian Ringneck, even the slightest friendly nibble can cause some serious damage.

These birds have a very strong biting ability and are known to easily crack the hardest nuts with great ease. Therefore, new owners should look for birds that have been handfed.

When they are younger, hand feeding these birds makes them used to the way our hands move. These birds are comfortable being handled and are less likely to perceive your fingers as a threat. It is also much easier to train these birds.

However, if you want to hand train the birds yourself, it is a good idea to bring home a baby. These birds are smaller and their bite will not hurt you as much. Of course, with younger birds, they are not as easily threatened. They tend to be more welcoming because of their curiosity towards new experiences.

For first time owners, handfed birds are the easier and safer options. If you adopt or want to bring home an adult bird who is not hand tamed, it is a good idea to look for a professional trainer who can help you train the bird.

What is a health certificate?

If you have decided which breeder you want to buy your Indian Ringneck from, the next step is to find out if they will give your bird a health certificate. Usually, a 90 day health certificate or guarantee is provided by the breeder. Some pet stores also provide these guarantees. If you know a local store that does, make sure that you make your purchase from there.

The health guarantee basically certifies that if your bird develops any health issues in this given time frame, then the breeder or the pet store will exchange the bird or give you all your money back. Now, these health guarantees come with a few conditions:

- The pet owner must have the bird checked by an Avian vet in less than 72 hours of purchase. In this checkup, if any health condition, genetic or otherwise is discovered, the breeder will give you a replacement.
- Any health issue that develops due to poor sanitation or nutrition in the given time span is not the responsibility of the breeder or the pet store.
- These stores or breeders will not pay for any veterinary costs including the first checkup. In fact, the first time you may have to approach a vet who has been suggested by the breeder or the pet store for the checkup to be valid. This is not a good sign as the vet and the breeder may be hand in hand in the entire process.
- Any accident or unfortunate incident will not be covered under this health guarantee.

The health guarantee only certifies that the bird that leaves the breeder or the pet store is in perfect condition. If there are any complications that develop under your care, you are solely responsible. Therefore, you need to make sure that you learn everything that you need to about these birds.

Certificate of Veterinary Inspection

If your birds are being shipped from the breeder's place or the pet store, make sure that you ask for a certificate of veterinary inspection. These certificates, also known as official health certificates, are necessary to ensure that your bird is not carrying any disease. These certificates are necessary in most states in the USA and in some parts of UK as well. These certificates are necessary when birds or any other livestock are entering a state for:

- A short visit
- Educational or research purposes
- Veterinary care
- A show or exhibition
- Sale as pets

If you fail to get this certificate for your bird, there are chances that he will not be allowed to pass customs. This experience can be stressful for the bird because there will be a lot of waiting and inspection that these birds absolutely dislike. You must also check if your bird needs any permit to be brought into your state.

2. Adopting an Indian Ringneck

Each year several birds are abandoned or dropped off at shelters for various reasons. Some of these birds are even rescued from abusive homes. Adopting an Indian Ringneck is one of the cheaper alternatives. However, you need to have some experience with parrots or other birds in order to deal with the possibility of any behavioral issues related to abuse and abandonment.

The first step to adopting an Indian Ringneck is to fill out an application form for adoption. This application form will ask for details about your profession, your experience with birds and also the reason for adoption.

Following this application form, you will be asked to take basic lessons about caring for Indian Ringnecks. These lessons could either be online or offline. You will also be given access to a lot of their educational material that you can refer to after taking the bird home. Many adoption agencies require that you complete a certain number of these basic classes before you are allowed to take a bird home.

After you have completed the required number of training hours, you will be allowed to take a tour of the aviary and the adoption center. That way, you get an idea about all the birds that are available for adoption. There are several cases when people decide that they want a certain bird but end up getting a different species altogether.

The idea is to form a bond with the right bird. Indian Ringnecks are birds with large personalities. If your personality does not match the bird's personality, you will have a tough time getting your bird to bond with you and actually want to be around you.

The last thing to do would be to visit the bird of your choice frequently. Once you have made up your mind to take a certain Indian Ringneck home, you need to let the bird get acquainted with you. You will also learn simple things like handling the bird, feeding him and cleaning the cage up etc. from the experts at the adoption agency.

Sometimes, it may so happen that you set your heart and mind on one bird who just does not seem to be interested. It is natural for that to happen. All you need to do is be patient with the bird and visit him as many times as you can.

When you are ready to take the bird home, most of these adoption centers will pay a visit to your home and will take care of all the little details required to help you get the bird settled into your home.

Now, if you already have pet birds at home, you will be required to present a full veterinary test result of each bird. This helps the agency ensure that the bird they are sending to your home does not have any vulnerability to fatal diseases. There are certain health standards that each of these agencies set for the health of your pet bird.

Are there any fees involved?

Most agencies and foundations will charge you an application fee that will include access to educational DVDs, toys and other assistance from the foundation.

You will also have to pay an adoption fee that may go up to $70 or £35 for an Indian Ringneck. These two separate fees are charged to make sure that you get all the assistance that you need with respect to making a positive start with your Indian Ringneck.

In addition to that, most agencies charge a rather high fee to ensure that the individuals who are investing in the bird are genuinely interested in having the bird. These fees will ward off people who want to just take the bird home for free with no clue about its care. Of course, you also need to consider the care provided to these birds while they are under the care of the foundation.

These fees cover all of that including the medical requirements of your bird. It is also the only source to pay the dedicated staff who take care of these abandoned or rescued birds day in and day out.

From the time you make the application for an Indian Ringneck, it takes about 6-10 weeks for it to be approved and for the bird to be sent to your home. Most of these centers will also have a probationary period of 90 days during which you will have to keep sending records of how the bird is progressing to them.

They will also pay home visits to ensure that the bird is being maintained well without any health issues. If the ambience or the facilities provided to the bird are not good enough, the bird will be taken back with no reimbursement of the adoption fee.

3. Male or female?

Now, with Indian Ringnecks, the females have a rather poor reputation. Now, these birds are more territorial and aggressive in the wild. However, when it comes to having them as pets, both of them are wonderful. What you need to know is that you must learn to deal with the different requirements of each gender.

In fact, females can make great pets. They are really good companions. These birds are even smarter than the males. Female Indian Ringnecks are extremely friendly and may get attached to the family easily. These birds also pick up more words than the male. This means that their vocabulary is also a lot higher. That makes them a lot of fun to be around. Females are also very easy to train. The only period when you need to be cautious is when the female is hormonal. During this period, she has the tendency to become very territorial.

That aside, female parrots are just as affectionate as the males. Most people believe that the male birds like to be cuddled while the female is a lot more independent. Like I mentioned before, these birds have strong personalities. Whether they like to cuddle or not depends on their personality. Some female Indian Ringneck owners claim that their girls love to snuggle and play with you.

It is said that female Indian Ringnecks are always on overdrive mentally. They love to solve puzzles, play with games, climb and just keep themselves entertained all day long. They are rebellious sometimes, which is why they have a reputation of being difficult to deal with. Some of these male birds just like to rest and sleep. With a female, you need to be careful as she is always up to something. These girls are mischievous, no doubt, but are definitely not notorious.

Talking is also a trait that is entirely dependent on the individual bird. You cannot say for sure that the females talk better than the males. Yes, they may learn more words. However, gender does not guarantee if your bird is going to be a speaker or not. Sometimes, a female Indian Ringneck may not even say a word!

Both male and female Indian Ringnecks are great companions. All you need to do is understand that these birds have massive personality differences. If you raise them from the time they are babies, you will be able to help them develop a personality that suits you and your family. However, if you bring a grown bird home, you need to calm down and just spend time with the bird. The more you are able to understand him or her you will realize that gender has no role to play in the personality and compatibility of an Indian Ringneck.

4. Fostering first

If you are a first time bird owner, consider fostering before you go to any of the sources mentioned above to obtain your bird.

Sometimes, you may have the opportunity to bring home a friend's bird. This could be because the owner is moving out or is unable to take care of the expenses associated with the bird. If you look in the newspaper adverts, you may find several people who need to find their pet a foster home.

If you are bringing a known person's bird home it is not an issue. However, if you plan to bring a stranger's bird home, you need to be prepared for a few difficulties initially. Some problems that foster parents face include:

Unwillingness to bond: Indian Ringnecks can get attached to the family that they live with. When you change their home and bring them amidst new people, they will miss their old "flock". This will lead to complications in the behavior of the bird. He may nip or bite whenever you try to interact. Indian Ringnecks develop problems with eating and also behavioral issues like feather plucking. It is advisable to spend a few months with the bird, in its old home before you actually bring him home. Ask the family if you can interact with their pet. That way, he will get to know you and will be more comfortable in your presence.

They may be hard to train and housebreak: Again, when you are fostering an Indian Ringneck, he or she is most likely to be an adult. This means that the bird already knows who he is and has a certain personality. Sometimes, this personality is very hard to break into. The bird may not like certain toys or certain foods. So, it will require a very experienced person to discipline the bird and make sure that he can live peacefully with his or her new family.

They may have health issues: Ask the owner why he wants to give the bird up, incase moving is not the reason. Sometimes, people who are unable to deal with the medical bills of their parrot will abandon him. So, you need to find out if the bird has any health issues. If you think that you can deal with health problems, you may bring the bird home. However, if you feel like it is too overwhelming, do not bring the bird into your home.

When you are bringing an Indian Ringneck home for foster care, make sure that you have the entire medical history of your bird at your disposal.

There is also a bright side to providing foster care. The bird is probably hand tamed already. This means that when the bird does housebreak eventually, he is easier to train unless any behavioral issues develop over time. You also know the temperament and behavior of the bird. So you know what to expect. The old owner's routine with the bird will help you set up your own routine with the bird quite easily. The previous owner also becomes a wonderful support system when you are raising the bird, if they have a good relationship with the bird.

Chapter 4: Housebreaking Indian Ringnecks

The term housebreaking has a different meaning with respect to parrots. It is often more complicated as these creatures are highly analytical. They need to be given extra care for them to feel comfortable and safe in their new environment. You must also remember that they do not care for too much interaction in the first few days of being in your home.

Housebreaking an Indian Ringneck basically requires you to let the bird take his time to observe. He will learn that this is his new flock with time and will show you some obvious signs that he is getting used to being around you. This chapter is all about understanding when and how to interact with a new bird that you bring home.

1. Day One

The first day of the bird in your home can be very hard on him or her. The transition from the breeders' or the adoption center to your home can be very strenuous. Indian Ringnecks, like any other bird, from the family of parrots dislike change and will be withdrawn and a little scared for the first few days. Here are a few tips to make this transition easy for your beloved new pet:

- When you are driving the bird home from the adoption center or from the breeders, keep your car quiet. Roll the windows up, set the air conditioner up to room temperature and place the cage of the bird in such a way that there are no bumps or movements. If your home is far away from the breeders' make sure that you stop frequently to let the bird relax. Do not talk to the bird or play loud music during the drive.

- Make sure that the housing for your bird is set up before you bring him home. Then, just place the door of the transfer cage towards the door of the bird's new home and wait for him to walk in.

- Make plenty of fresh water and food available to the bird. In case your bird has been on a seed diet at the breeders' do not try to change it right away. You can make the changes after the bird is accustomed to the new environment. In the meantime, it is alright to introduce a few fruits and fresh vegetables to your bird and see how he responds.

- The cardinal rule on day one is to leave the bird alone. Let him try to understand his new surroundings first. He will most probably not even allow you to handle him. This is natural as your bird has still not formed that bond with you.

- It is tempting to show off a bird as beautiful as the Indian Ringneck. You can invite a friend or two over to just observe the bird from afar. Even if you have people who are experienced with birds, make sure that the Indian Ringneck is not handled by them. That will make the bird anxious and uncomfortable.

- Sleeping might be an issue as the sights and sounds of your home are new for the bird. Make sure that he is away from the television that can keep him up for longer hours. Placing a cloth over the cage will give your bird a nice resting spot.

- Do not interact too much with the bird on the first day. A hello in the softest voice possible is the only thing you can do. Never tower over the cage. Instead, stay at eye level with the bird at all times. This makes them feel like an equal and not like a prey animal.

Allow the bird to just observe you and your family for the first day. The lesser you interact with him, the better it is. You can even ask the breeder to give you a favorite toy of the bird to take home with you. This is a familiar object that will help the bird calm down. The time that a bird takes to open up to you and become more interactive depends entirely on the personality of the bird.

2. Making the bird comfortable

Remember that every voice in your household is something entirely new for the bird. Let the bird get used to this for a few days. Placing the cage in an area that allows the bird to watch over without getting disturbed is the best thing to do.

Take the first few days to develop a routine with your bird. The first thing you will do after you wake up each morning is clean out the food and water bowls and feed your bird. You can spend some time with your hands on the sides of the cage while the bird is feeding. Make sure you are at eye level.

After a few days, the curious Indian Ringneck will try to peck at your hand and just get a feel of what it is. Don't force it upon the bird. Let him come to you instead of the other way around.

Then get on with your chores. Make sure your bird is able to see you. When you enter the room that the bird is placed in just greet him with a hello and say goodbye when you leave the room. This should be practiced by everyone in the family so that the bird gets acquainted with the voice.

For the first few days, do not allow anyone else to feed the bird. This should be done by the person who got the bird home. When your bird forms a bond with you, it is safer to introduce him to the other members in your family.

Lastly, the first few days are very crucial to determine if your bird is showing signs of any behavioral or physical problems. So, observe the bird carefully. If you see that there is any change from what is normal such as too much water consumption, lack of energy, staggering while walking, heavy breathing, lack of appetite or even excessive aggression, it might be a good idea to consult the vet. That way, any problem can be fixed in the initial stages so that you can enjoy the rest of your journey with your Indian Ringneck.

3. Lay down some ground rules

This is definitely an exciting time for your family. They are going to have a new pet that they believe they can play with and have a good time with. Of course, that will be possible with time. Indian Ringnecks also have a good reputation for being able to talk well and play for several hours with their owners. However, for the first few days, you need to make sure that everyone in your family follows certain rules with respect to the bird:

- **No touching or even approaching:** For the first few weeks, no one will approach the bird, tap at the cage or even talk to it. In fact, you should not do that yourself. The only interaction that you have with your bird must be limited to feeding and cleaning till he gets used to the new home and the new environment. New voices, new faces and even the new colors in your home can be very stressful for your bird. They may react by biting or just developing a lot of fear.

- **No visitors:** The Indian Ringneck is a gorgeous bird. So, it is natural for you to want to show off your new pet. Wait until the bird is well socialized to do this. People who see your bird will react with appreciative comments like "Wow!" "What an amazing bird!"etc in an excited voice. This is very disturbing to a parrot. Your Indian Ringneck may also react to a hat or a moustache in a very negative way. Allow him to settle in first before you actually bring home any guests or visitors. If you do have people coming over to see the bird, make sure they do it from afar, silently.

- **No loud music or sound:** If your Indian Ringneck has been exposed to sounds like the TV or radio at the breeder's it is easier for you. Even then, make sure that these appliances do not run too loudly for the first week. If you want to use them, keep the Indian Ringneck in a place where the sound will not reach them. You may also close the door to the room. If you love to host parties, remember that this is a complete no-no for at least a fortnight from the time your bird comes home.

- **No feeding:** Unlike cats and dogs, birds do not respond positively to feeding. This is something you have to tell your family well in advance. Only one person will take the responsibility of feeding the bird and cleaning the cage for the first few days. No one will go ahead and feed the bird in an untimely fashion. This can spoil the routine of the bird and also make him unhealthy.

Your whole family should have some knowledge about the bird that you are about to bring home. Encourage them to read up about the behavior of the bird and also the requirements of the bird. With the right kind of behavior, you can ensure that your bird is less stressed. That way, the housebreaking process is easier on him.

4. Do you have other pets?

If you have other birds or pets such as a cat or a dog, you need to remember that the introduction is the most crucial part of helping them get along and share your home cordially.

Introducing your new bird to other birds

The first step to introducing new birds is to have the bird quarantined for 30 days at least. This gives you enough time to observe the bird for any signs of infection that could be contagious. To quarantine the new bird, you need to keep him or her in a separate cage, in a separate room. Birds will get acquainted with one another thanks to their loud calls. So, you can expect your pet birds to be ready for a new member during the introduction.

It is never a good idea to place birds of different sizes in the same cage. The larger bird might become more dominating, putting the smaller bird at great risk. If you have an aviary with birds about the same size as the Indian Ringnecks, such as the Cockatoo, you could keep them together. However, there is no guarantee that your birds will be friendly with each other and will take to each other's company.

During the actual introduction, you will introduce your Indian Ringneck to the least dominant bird in the flock. You can first start by placing them in separate cages side by side. You can also get a new cage that they both can be placed in, in order to reduce territorial behavior. If the birds just mind their own business and do not attack one another, you can consider it a successful introduction. You can progress to the more dominant birds in the same fashion.

These introductions will only happen in your presence so that you can observe the behavior of the birds. When you are introducing the more dominant birds to your Indian Ringneck, it is best to do it in a more open space like the living room. This gives the bird ample room to run away or fly away if there is any sign of aggression from the other one.

After you are certain that these individual introductions went well, you can place the bird in the aviary. Watch the reaction of the other birds carefully. If you notice that one of them retreats completely, it is a sign that he or she is not happy with the new member in the group. On the other hand, if you see your Indian Ringneck being chased around the cage, he could be in danger of attacks and wounds.

Birds may get along with no traces of jealousy or dominance at times. But if this does not happen in your home despite several attempts, it is not a matter of great disappointment. Sometimes, birds may just not get along with one another. That is when you place them in separate cages and leave them alone.

This ensures that no bird is harmed unnecessarily. You will also prevent a great deal of stress that the bird may go through when he is introduced to another bird who is so hostile or even aggressive in some cases.

Indian Ringnecks, Cats and Dogs

Cats and dogs are predators by the natural order. That already makes them a threat to your Indian Ringneck irrespective of how sweet and friendly they are towards people.

During the first few days, allow the bird to become aware of the presence of the other animal. Let him watch and observe your pet cat or dog. There must be no surprises later on. Just make sure that your dog or cat does not approach the cage while you are away. Your cat, especially, should not be allowed to climb over the cage.

When the bird seems settled in, it is time for the introductions. While keeping the bird in the cage, you will let the dog or cat around it. Let them sniff and explore. If your dog begins to bark or if your cat becomes aggressive, separate them instantly.

Now, keep doing this until your dog or cat is used to the bird. That will make them ignore the new member of the family even when in the same room. When you have reached this stage, it may be safe to let the bird out and interact with the pets

You can take this liberty only when your dog or cat has been trained well to heel. When these animals are trained, the risk to the bird is reduced to a large extent as you will be able to control your cat or dog even if they just get too excited.

If you see that your pet cat or dog is chasing the bird around, you must put the bird back in the cage. In case your bird is not hand trained, wrap a towel around his body and your hands while handling him.

In any case, it is never advisable to leave the bird alone with your pets. While they may seem to get along with each other perfectly well in your presence, do not take any risks.

A dog can seriously harm the Indian Ringneck with a simple friendly nibble. At the same time, your Indian Ringneck can rip the dog's ear right off when provoked. As for cats, the biggest threat is the saliva of the cat, which is poisonous for an Indian Ringneck.

Remember that you are dealing with highly instinctive creatures. You can never be sure of when their instinctive behavior will kick in. So, it is best that you let them interact in your presence. In case there are any signs of aggression, it is best to keep your Indian Ringneck confined in the presence of the cat or the dog.

5. Socializing and learning to handle the bird

In the case of Indian Ringnecks, socializing means more than just being friendly around people. Unlike cats and dogs, you must not expect your bird to be friendly with just about anyone. They take time to open up to people. There is a very valid reason for this. Parrots have been domesticated for a few hundred years. They are not genetically inclined to being around people. However, cats and dogs have been domesticated for ages, making them better at socializing. With parrots, socializing is a multi-layered process.

The first thing you need to do is get your bird to accept change. Yes, a routine is very important. But, the bird needs to be more adaptable. A good way of doing this is by having two cages for the bird. One for the indoors and one for when you take him outside to play. Changing cages makes the birds less territorial. You can even shift the location of the cage from time to time to ensure that the bird is comfortable in new surroundings.

The next thing is to establish flock behavior with your bird. This must include your whole family. Try to have at least one meal with your parrot. Time it in such a way that your parrot is able to see you eating while he eats. Encourage him to try new foods. The more variety of foods he eats, the more adaptable he is going to be. One interesting thing about parrots is that they will only try new foods when they see someone else eat that food and be okay. Encourage the bird to try out a new food item. You just need to be over expressive about how good a certain food is.

Try to make noises like, "Yummmmmmm!" or tell the bird how good the food is. Of course, he is not going to get the meaning of what you are trying to say. But he will recognize a positive tone. Take some food from your plate and put it into the bowl (make sure this is a food recommended in the Indian Ringneck diet). He will try to eat it. Of course, sharing food is a great form of bonding as parrots only share food with their mates or babies in the wild. Now, don't be surprised if your bird throws up some food in front of you as an offering. This is him giving you some love back.

When you want to introduce your parrot to people, take it slow. First, let the bird just see your guests hanging out in the living room or the dining room. Allow the guests to walk around the cage. Let the bird observe. Then, you may introduce your friends to the bird in a soft tone. Ask them not to talk to the bird until he has seen them come in and out a few times. Handling the bird is only allowed when he is ready. If you want the parrot to get along with one of your best friends, they need to start off just the way you did. This rule applies for anyone who wishes to handle your bird.

Chapter 5: Caring for your Indian Ringneck

There are three very important aspects of providing good care for your bird; food, healthcare and cleanliness. All three are needed to prevent any illness and to make sure that your bird is happy.

This chapter explains each aspect of care in great detail to help you ensure that you are giving your bird exactly when he requires.

1. What to feed Indian Ringnecks?

These birds absolutely love fresh fruits. They may even take to vegetables, although they will prefer the former. When you are giving your bird any fruit, make sure it is fully ripe. If the fruit is too ripe and close to spoiling, do not give it to your bird. This eliminates any 'seconds' from your local grocery store.

No matter what fruit or veggies you give the bird, wash it thoroughly to prevent any infection due to pesticides. The food that your parrot consumes should be free from any chemicals. It is a good idea to get a food bowl that is about 6 cm deep and about 12.5 cm wide. Filling this to the brim with fresh fruits and veggies is a good portion for the bird.

If you want to include pellets in the bird's diet, make sure that it makes the first meal. Then, you will have to add fresh pellets into the bird's food bowl in the morning and provide a few pieces of fruits and vegetables at around mid-morning and evening. With pellets, you need to again ensure that they are given in good moderation because they are usually fortified and packed with several nutrients.

Do not forget about the treats that you are giving your bird. Getting treats like "Nutriberries" may be a good option when the bird does not need as many treats. Initially, stick to the natural treats such as sunflower seeds or nuts, especially for an Indian Ringneck.

Ideally, your Indian Ringneck's meal must consist of 60% fresh produce, 20% legumes and 20% pellets.

Usually, the diet of the bird remains the same throughout the year. However, during molting season and breeding season, you need to be very careful about what you feed the bird to ensure maximum nutrition. We will discuss about the feed required in the breeding season in the following chapters.

The molting season is a stressful time for the bird. This starts when the bird is about 8 months old. They begin to lose their old feathers which are replaced by new, fresh ones. With birds like the Indian Ringneck that is quite a heavy moulter, a lot of energy is consumed in this process. Protein is an essential element for molting to take place. After all, the feather is made of keratin which is a form of protein. So if there isn't enough consumption of protein, the bird will be lethargic and tired at all times.

You also need to know that these birds are very irritable in this season. Poor nutrition only adds to this bad behavior of the bird. If you increase protein levels, especially, you will see that the bird is happier and less stressed.

What foods NEVER to give

Any part of an avocado is toxic for the bird. You must also never give the bird any apple seeds, rhubarb and seeds from the stone fruit. Lettuce is alright in very small proportions. However, it can dehydrate your bird severely. Onion, raw meat, garlic, cheese, chocolate, coffee, soft drinks and alcohol can severely damage the health of your bird. Birds can be lactose intolerant. So, avoid any dairy products. Fatty foods or even take away food like Chinese will have a lot of preservatives like MSG and artificial flavors. These chemicals can be harmful for your bird in the long run. Keep the foods as natural as possible, especially for Indian Ringnecks.

Is supplementation required?

All Indian Ringneck owners will tell you that these birds require more Vitamin A in comparison to all the other species of birds. If you give them a bowl of fruits, you will see that these birds will instinctively move towards the foods that are rich in Vitamin A such as sweet potatoes, peppers, kale, cantaloupe and other red or orange fruits and veggies.

That said, it is a good idea to give the birds natural sources of vitamin A instead of supplements unless your bird has any Vitamin A related health issues. Before you give your parrot any supplements, make sure that you consult your avian vet.

Calcium supplements may be recommended for your bird. This is only when you see severe calcium deficiency symptoms such as weakness of the bones, skeletal deformities, spayed legs, stunted growth, deformities in the beak, weakened muscles and weight loss. These supplements are usually given to birds when they are younger. You also need to increase calcium in the diet of a brooding hen to ensure that the shell is properly formed.

2. Sanitation

We have spoken about cage maintenance in the previous chapter. The next thing to do is to make sure that your bird is well-groomed. Grooming has more than one benefit. Not only does it keep your bird clean and healthy, it also improves the bond that you have with your bird. Some grooming activities are also essential for the safety of your bird.

Bathing

Parrots love to bathe themselves. If you leave an extra bowl of water in the cage, you will see the bird bathing itself or at least picking water up with its beak and preening itself. Your bird will keep himself clean by preening. If they are in a pair, you will see that they preen each other. However, giving your bird a bath every fortnight is a great bonding exercise. It also keeps the bird clean.

The best thing to do is to mist the bird with some warm water. You can use a spray bottle and gently spray some water on the body, making sure that you do not get any on the eyes directly. If you see that the bird is cringing or trying to get away, it means that he is not enjoying the bath and you need to stop immediately.

You could also use a bird bath. Make sure that the water is shallow enough for your bird to walk around. An effective method to draw a bird to the bath is to place a few spinach leaves in the water. While the bird forages, he will also give himself a bath. Of course, a hand tamed bird can be gently lowered into the water bath. If he shows any signs of fear or anxiety, it is a good idea to get him out of there instantly.

You must avoid using soap or detergent of any kind. You may use a recommended mild soap only if there is any hardened grime or mud that you need to get rid of immediately. After the bird has taken a bath, let him dry off naturally. It is not necessary to use a hair dryer unless it is too cold. Of course, turn the air conditioning off when the bird is drying himself. Then, the bird will preen the feathers into place and look as good as new.

Wing Clipping

Some people believe that wing clipping is not ethically correct. If you are one of them, make sure that your home is a safe haven for your bird. You do not want to have any flight related accidents at home. This may also lead to escape and loss of your precious Indian Ringneck.

If you have pets at home, do not clip the wings. This is your bird's only form of defense. Even when you have multiple birds in an aviary, the wings should be intact to help your bird escape an aggressive cage mate.

If you decide to clip your bird's wings, make sure you have it done at the vet's the first time. You can learn how to do it, practice with your vet and then do it at home. You need to be very experienced to ensure that you do not accidentally get any blood feathers.

A bird must be hand tamed before you decide to clip his wings yourself. He must be comfortable enough to let you handle him. The first thing is to get your bird into a comfortable position to clip his wings. Pick him up using a towel and place him face down on your thigh. Then let the first wing out of the loose end of the towel and spread the feathers. Cut the primary feathers only. These are the largest feathers. The first three feathers are usually cut. You can snip about 1cm from each feather.

Then, repeat on the other side. Compare the wings to make sure that they are equal. If they are not, your bird will have difficulty walking or even perching. In case you do get a blood feather, make sure you apply styptic power to the wound immediately. If the bleeding does not stop, take the pet to the vet to have the shaft removed off.

Clipping the wings only reduces your bird's ability to fly. It does not prevent flight altogether. So, when you take your bird outdoors, be vigilant. Even the slightest breeze can give him the lift he needs and lead to an escape. You need to clip the wings every 6 months. With these playful birds, trimming of toe nails or beaks is not needed as they will do it themselves by scraping the sharp surfaces off on any rough object like the wooden perch.

Toe and beak trimming

This grooming process is optional. If you notice that your bird's toes and beak are getting stuck in the toys or any fabric, you can trim them to avoid any accidents. If the beak or toe of your bird is stuck to the fabric on your upholstery and he tries to move suddenly, there are chances that the whole toe is ripped off or the beak is severely damaged. To avoid this, trim the sharp ends.

Wrap the bird with a towel, only exposing the part that you want to trim. In the case of the beak, gently lift the upper mandible with your finger and feel the sharp end. Keep the beak supported and trim the beak using a nail file. When you feel that it is just blunt, stop trimming. If the nail or the toe is too short, the bird will be unable to climb and hold properly.

Even with the toe, make sure that you have a finger supporting the nail you want to trim to avoid any chances of breakage or unwanted damage.

It is a good idea to give your bird perches and toys of different textures. That will let the nails and the beak stay blunt naturally. As the bird climbs or chews with the proper toys, the beak and nails get trimmed. You will see them rubbing their beak onto rough surfaces as an attempt to keep them trimmed. This is an instinctive practice that should be encouraged.

Remember that bonding with birds as intelligent as parrots requires a lot of effort from your end. These birds will analyze every situation that they are put into and even the slightest doubt will break their trust. If you have adopted a bird that has been abused, this will take longer. You will also need a lot of assistance from your avian vet to gain the trust of such birds. Take it one step at a time and make sure that you do not rush him.

Worming

The intestinal tract of your bird needs worming on a regular basis. These birds may develop internal parasites that make the bird very unwell if left unnoticed. This deterioration in health is ongoing if you do not set up a good worming routine for your bird.

Now, the worms usually get into a bird's tract when they ingest the droppings of other birds accidentally. These droppings may contain worms. Now, even if your bird is not exposed to wild birds or the outdoors, worming is necessary. He may consume these worms through dirt brought in with our shoes or even when we use natural perches in the cage.

You will get wormers in pet pharmacies. The most recommended ones are Wormout Gel and Avitrol Plus. You may add these wormers to the water bowl every three months to keep the intestines free from parasites.

When you make a worming routine, keep the following things in mind:

- You should not worm a bird who us underweight.
- Moist foods must be avoided when you worm the bird.
- Never worm them on very hot days as the birds may consume less water because of the medicine.
- Consult your vet before providing your bird with any wormer.
- Keep alternating between different brands to make sure that the parasites do not become immune to the medicines.

With these simple grooming practices, you will have a healthy bird at home. You will also notice that grooming activities inculcate trust in the bird and make your bond stronger.

3. Healthcare

Your bird needs a good avian vet. You need to find one even before you bring the bird home so that you can get all the assistance that you need in case you hit a roadblock with your bird. Sometimes, birds can develop serious health issues when you are breaking them into a new home. And, finding the right help is necessary because all vets are not trained to treat birds. You will have to find an avian vet who specializes in the anatomy of these creatures and has experience with the various health issues that they face.

Who is an avian vet?

An avian vet is someone who is specialized in providing medical care for birds. He or she may even have studied exotic species of birds as part of their course. Their practice also includes several hours of work with facilities that deal especially with birds. Most avian vets are members of the Association of Avian Vets. If you can find one who is a member, it is great. However, you could even have an avian vet who is not a part of it because he or she has not worked with birds that are of a very rare species.

If your breeder can recommend a good avian vet, it is convenient. However, if you feel like you need more options because this clinic is inaccessible or you are not satisfied with the facility, you may even ask for details in a local bird club, an online bird forum, a pet store or even in the clinic of a vet dealing with animals like cats and dogs. One reliable source to find all the contact details of avian vets from across the USA is the Association of Avian Vets. You can visit their website www.aav.org or call their central office in Florida on 407-393-8901. Once you have the details, make sure you personally visit the clinic to ensure that your bird will be in safe hands.

Choosing the right one

You need to ask the avian vet that you have chosen a few important questions. This will give you a fair idea about the experience and the commitment of the facility towards the well-being of your bird. Remember, you need to be able to sustain the relationship with your avian vet for a really long time. So, find someone who is compatible and approachable. Here are a few questions that you can ask the vet during the interview:

Do you treat only birds?

Sometimes, avian vets may also treat other species of animals that are exotic. This includes reptiles and a few rodents too. In that case, find out how much of the practice is dedicated to birds? If the vet is only taking care of 3-4 birds in a week or month, then you may have to look for more options as the facility may not specialize in birds.

How do they stay updated?

Avian medicine is a fast changing field. One needs to stay updated by attending seminars, reading journals etc. Ask your vet if he is associated with any clubs or if he attends any conferences or seminars regularly. Ask him with an intention of participating in one yourself. If your vet is willing to take time off to learn about the birds, he is certainly committed towards providing the best care for your bird.

How experienced are the staff?

You should be able to guess this by the behavior of the staff members towards you and your bird. If they are uncomfortable handling the cage or the bird, they are definitely not experienced. You need to make sure that everyone, including the front office, is friendly towards the birds.

How long does each appointment last?

This will help you decide if the vet is thorough in the examination or not. If you are only going to get 15-20 mins, it means that the facility is not up to the mark. They need to get the bird out of the cage and perform a thorough check up. That is when you know for sure that they are doing a good job. This will take at least 30-45 minutes per bird.

Is he available 24X7?

Emergencies never give you a warning. So, you need to know some way of accessing medical assistance 24X7. If your vet does not have such a facility, he will at least be associated with one that is good and reliable.

Do they have hostels to admit the bird?

Ask them how they would care for a bird that needs to be admitted, probably post-surgery. They should be associated with a hostel that helps them with this. Of course, some facilities have their own little wards for the birds. Make sure that the birds are kept in individual cages in clean and hygienic conditions.

Signs of concern

If you observe one or more of the following signs, you need to try and find a new facility for your bird:

- The staff is unable to provide you with any instructions over the phone in case of an emergency. They will not even be able to provide advice about bringing your bird to the vet when it is too cold or too hot outside.

- The staff members do not know how to handle birds.

- Weighing the birds is not a regular practice when you take them in for a checkup.
- The vet examines the bird whilst in the cage.
- Diet is not an important subject of discussion when your bird is unwell.

- They do not have basic facilities such as incubators or gram scales.

Chapter 6: Bonding with your Indian Ringneck

Indian Ringnecks form extremely strong bonds with their owners. It does take some effort from your end to make the bond stronger each day. These birds simply love to play and spend time with their owners. Sure, you cannot expect too many cuddles, but the idea that your bird just loves interacting with you is extremely satisfying.

With birds as intelligent as the Indian Ringneck, there is never a dull moment. You can really enjoy playtime, teach them new tricks and above all, teach them how to talk.

This chapter talks about different things that you can do to make your journey with your Indian Ringneck exciting. From learning how to read the body language of your bird to advanced bird training, here is everything that you need to know.

1. Learn the body language

Birds rely heavily on their body postures to communicate the way they are feeling. You can easily tell whether your bird is happy, angry, bored, tired or unwell just by looking at the posture. Here are a few body language tips that every Indian Ringneck owner must know about:

The body
- If your bird is on your shoulder and is constantly tugging on the collar of your shirt, it means that he wants to get off.
- If the head of the bird is lowered while the wings are lifted slightly, he wants you to pick him up.
- If the bird is hanging with one or both feet from the cage, he is in a playful mood.
- If his rear end rubs the table while he walks back, he is going to take a poop.

The eyes
- All parrots exhibit pinning which is rapid dilation of the pupils. This is either done when the bird is excited or when the bird is afraid. You can study the situation to tell how your bird is feeling.

The voice
- If the bird is talking, whistling or singing, it means that he is happy and quite content.
- If he is mumbling to himself or is just chattering softly, he is practicing the words that he learnt.
- Loud chatter is considered attention seeking behavior.
- Clicking of the tongue means that the bird is just entertaining himself or is calling you to play with him.
- Growling is a sign of aggression. There could be something in the room that is bothering him. Removing that object will make him stop immediately.

The beak
- If you notice your bird grinding his beak just before he sleeps, it means that he is very happy to be in your home.
- Clicking of the beak when you pass by is your bird's way of greeting you. At the same time, clicking when you are holding him means that he does not want to be handled by you at the moment.
- If the beak is on the ground and the feathers are fluffed, he wants you to pet him.
- If your Indian Ringneck regurgitates, it is a sign of great affection. They do this only for their mates in the wild.
- Bobbing the head is a type of attention seeking behavior.
- If the bird is just rubbing his beak on the perch, he is cleaning himself.

Feet and legs
- If your bird is standing upright with his weight equally on both feet, he is content and happy.
- If the posture of the bird is upright and he is looking at you, it means that he wants you to pick him up right that instant.
- If the bird is feeling restless and impatient, he will rock back and forth on the perch.
- If the bird is standing on one foot, he is relaxed.
- If he is standing on one foot with all his feathers fluffed, he is happy.
- If your bird is standing on one foot and has the beak tucked beneath the wing, he is just cleaning himself.

- If he is standing on one foot but is grinding his beak, he is tired.
- If he is standing on one foot with glazed eyes and semi-fluffed feathers, it means that he is falling asleep.
- If the bird is scratching the bottom of the cage, he wants you to let him out.
- Tapping of the feet indicates that the bird is trying to protect his or her territory.

The feathers
- Ruffled feathers can mean one of the following things:
    - The bird is feeling too cold and is trying to warm himself up.
    - The bird is trying to relieve tension and stress.
    - The bird is sick.
    -

Position of the crest
- If the crest is lifted, the bird is excited.
- If the crest is puffed up it is seen as a sign of aggression.
- If the crest is flat on the ground while the bird is hissing, it means that he is scared or just getting ready to attack someone.

The tail
- If the tail is shaking, the bird is preparing for some fun times ahead.
- Tail bobbing means that the bird is tired or is catching his breath after strenuous physical activity. If this behavior is seen even when the bird has not done anything physically demanding, you need to take him to a vet immediately.
- Fanning of the tail is usually a sign of aggression. The bird is displaying his strength through this body language.

Wings
- Flapping of the wings is an attention seeking behavior.
- Flipping of the wings could indicate one or more of the following:
    - Pain or discomfort
    - Anger and aggression
    - A call for your attention.
- If the wings of your bird are drooping it is generally a sign that the bird is unwell.

The head

- If the head is turned back and tucked below the wing, your bird is asleep.
- When the head is lowered and turned, your bird finds something very interesting.
- If the head is down and the wings are extended, your bird is just stretching or yawning.

These simple behavior patterns will help you choose the best time to form that bond with your beloved pet. Responding aptly to this body language also helps the bird trust you more because you are one of his own now.

2. Building trust

The first step towards bonding is building trust with your parrot. As mentioned before, these birds are very intelligent and can really analyze situations. So, unless they trust you, they will not form a close bond. Unlike dogs and cats, these creatures do not respond to feeding. You cannot expect to just feed your parrot and get him to like you. It is a slow process that can be quite frustrating for some pet owners.

If you know that your bird has been hand tamed, your work is reduced quite considerably. These birds will not perceive your hands as a threat and will be more approachable. However, if the parrot has not been hand tamed, do not grab him or try to handle him. You will definitely be bitten. And the bite of a parrot can be really nasty. Think of jamming your finger in a door hinge. That is how painful it is.

So, if your Indian Ringneck is not hand tamed, the first step is to start letting him out of the cage. This should be done in a safe environment without any other pets or any running electrical appliances, especially fans. Start by target training practice. This is useful for both hand tamed parrots and non-hand tamed parrots.

Target training

Give your bird a target to follow. Start with a chopstick or even a plastic stick. Bring it close to the bird's beak and say "Touch". If the bird touches the target, make a clicking noise with your mouth and offer a treat. You can even get a hand held clicker. Mouth clicking is convenient. Do this a couple of times until the bird will touch the target immediately upon seeing it. The clicking sound followed by the treat will make him associate the clicking sound with positive reinforcement.

Then, you can change the target and offer your fingers. Do not start off with the finger as you do not know how hard the bird may bite the first time. You know that your bird is target trained when you can lead him around the cage easily. Now, open the cage door and lead the parrot out with the target. Allow him to explore the area outside. He may climb up the cage and just walk around. When you want to put him back, lead him in with the target and give him a treat or his favorite toy. The treat or toy will tell him that going back to the cage is a good thing.

Also, since you are giving the bird a treat, he will also begin to like you. You know that your bird trusts you when he becomes fully upright on seeing you and seems almost anxious to be with you. This may take a few weeks or maybe just a few hours. Each bird is unique. So give them time.

3. Playing with the bird

Playing and mental stimulation is not just a source of entertainment, it is a necessity for parrots. Many people will try to tell you that the Indian Ringneck is lethargic and boring. This is completely false. A bird that is too quiet and lazy is a bird that is either unwell or extremely lazy. All parrots are intelligent and need to be stimulated mentally to make sure that they are healthy. Each parrot has a different style of play and understanding that will help you devise fun games and activities.

Style of play

Foraging is one of the Indian Ringneck's most favorite forms of play. They will simply love the foraging toys that you can buy at stores. If you plan to give them these toys, be prepared to replace them often. Indian Ringnecks are very smart and will figure the toy out in no time. Once that happens, foraging is no longer fun. That is when your creativity comes to play. Make sure that you include foraging activities in their routine. This could mean looking for a treat in some gap in one of the old toys, some corner of the cage etc. They will really enjoy the experience of hunting down their favorite treat.

One form of play that we often neglect is "observation". Parrots love to watch people and imitate them. They will listen to your conversations very intently. So, once your parrot is accustomed to your home, you need to spend time talking to him. Honestly, it feels like you are talking to another human being.

Toys that make noises are also appreciated by Indian Ringnecks. They get really excited when you give them toys that make a sound upon pushing some button or when you move the toy. You can actually pass a few of your child's toys to the parrot and watch him get just as excited as your baby. If you plan to use children's toys, make sure that the casing is very sturdy and that the batteries do not fall out easily. The battery is toxic for your little bird. It should also not have small parts that the parrot may swallow.

Basically, parrots love the idea of manipulating objects with their beaks. This includes untying knots, twisting knobs or just playing with beads. As long as it is fiddly and time consuming, your bird will love it.

Do they like to move around?

If the parrot is in the cage for most part of the day, he is likely to stick to the top of the cage or the perch. They will seldom go on the floor and pick up a toy that they like. In a confined space, an Indian Ringneck will try to take the easy way out. You will see that the bird will try to hang from the perch and just reach for the toy. They will try to return to the perch as soon as possible even if they do get off for a bit.

But if you give the parrots space, i.e. a bigger cage or some time outdoors, movement is a very important part of play. The bird will try to scatter his toys around, they will climb and even fly from one toy to another and generally explore the place. If the cage is big enough, adding multiple perches or swings will encourage the bird to move around more. This will make your bird a lot healthier because he will get ample exercise and physical movement.

Are they destructive?

Indian Ringnecks are usually not destructive. However, there are times when they just like to get a little crazy and chew their heart out. This

71

destructive behavior is targeted towards softer objects like thread, paper or leaves that they can shred with their sharp beaks.

If you have wooden toys or objects in the cage, the parrot will go for the softer woods like Balsa. They will just leave hard surfaces alone. So, if you want to keep the perch intact, it is a good idea to have it made from birch, maple and other hard woods. The rule with parrots is simple- if it does not break, it is no fun!

Drawn to the string

If you have several beads and toys hanging in the cage, don't be surprised if your parrot heads for the material used to string the toy rather than the toy itself. They like to pull and tug at this material and sort of separate the tufts. They cannot resist knots and will try to untie them.

This is fun to watch but also has a downside. Most of the toys will be pulled down on a regular basis. You need to have thicker thread. That puts a limitation on the beads that you can use. Most parrot beads are meant for small threads.

You can just make up for this behavior by keeping stringing material handy. If not, you can use chains or steel wires to suspend the toys. They are both quite expensive. But, you can avoid damage to the toys that are even more expensive. Eventually, you will figure out which toys attract the bird towards the knot and which toys attract the bird towards the beads and other play elements. Once that is done, you can place the appropriate toy in the cage and avoid unwanted destruction.

What makes them unhappy?

Don't think that you will never go wrong with toys and play. There are some things that your Indian Ringneck will absolutely hate. Swings, for example, are not readily accepted by these birds. These toys are wobbly and the bird may have small mishaps with them. In any case, an Indian Ringneck does not appreciate new things thrown into the cage. They will approach anything new with a lot of caution, including toys.

So, when you place a swing, the parrot may avoid it initially. The good thing about Indian Ringnecks is that they are really quick learners. They will be able to learn to balance themselves on the swing with regular practice. Do not force it upon them. Let them just enjoy the whole experience and take it one step at a time.

If you are bringing new toys for your bird, don't just place it in the cage. They do not appreciate new toys unlike cats and dogs. As mentioned before, these birds are contemplative. You must leave the toy outside the cage and let the bird just watch it for a while and explore it at its own pace when you let him out. If his reaction to this is positive, you can place it in the cage. If not, just avoid it.

Do not bring toys with big gaps and holes till your parrot is a little more skilled at using toys. This could lead to the head or the toes getting stuck in the gap, making the bird averse to toys altogether.

Toys

The market is flooded with several toys that you can buy for your bird. These toys are either available online or can be bought from your local pet store. Here are some fun options for your bird:

- **Foraging barrels:** You can place treats inside these barrels and let your bird just look for them and pick them out. These barrels are rather deep and are fun for your bird. You will get these barrels in various sizes to suit your parrot.

- **Claw reels:** You will get ready made cotton or plastic reels that can be suspended with a steel wire. These toys are handled by the birds using their claws. They simply love these soft and cushy reels that can be pulled and twisted.

- **Bells:** You can get special nickel plated hanging bells that are sturdy. These bells are usually made from the same material used to make bullet proof glass. These toys are noisy, can be pulled around and are very entertaining for your bird.

- **Leather towers:** Special chewing towers are made for your bird using leather. You can even make this at home by piling up layers of leather that is vegetable tanned. These towers are shredded and practically destroyed by the bird. You can even make a similar tower using palm leaves that your bird will love to shred into pieces. If this is not interesting, paper also works as a brilliant substitute.

You can get several other toys such as pacifiers that are made from beads and strings. Your Indian Ringneck is sure to love these toys. Just make sure that it is safe, free from any lead or lead based paint and durable. Make sure that the toys do not have a zinc plate either. This is very dangerous for your bird. Twine should never be used to hang the toys as it can cause cuts when the bird is flying around in the cage. No sharp edges in the cage- this is a rule that every parrot owner must follow to keep his beloved pet safe and secure.

Homemade toys and puzzles

Toys can get expensive. With a bird like the Indian Ringneck, it is impossible to keep them pleased with the same old toy. They tend to get bored with toys that they have used several times. They do not even like toys that are "too easy". Remember, you are dealing with a highly intelligent creature. You need to get twice as creative if you want to keep them entertained.

You can make several toys at home to keep the bird interested. One of the easiest things to do is a foraging box. All you need to do is get a small box, seal it from all ends with just one end open. Then, stuff it with shredded paper and hide treats amidst the paper. Watch your bird forage around and have a great time. These boxes can even be suspended to make playtime more interesting for your bird.

If you do not have the time, you can simply wrap a paper tower with treats, add some layers and throw it into the cage. The bird will just rip the paper towel apart in pursuit of his favorite toy.

Bottle caps make very interesting toys for your bird. You can string a couple of them together and suspend them in the cage. The bird will tug and pull at these colorful caps. You can even hide a treat under one of the bottle caps and keep two empty ones. Shuffle the caps around and let your bird pick the one with the treat. This is great fun even for you.

If you are a wine lover, you are sure to have several corks lying around. Stitch a thread through the cork using a large needle. Make a few holes on the cork and stuff seeds into it. Hang this in the cage and your bird is sure to fall in love with it.

Besides this, you can use blocks of soft wood, paper and even leaves as chew toys for the bird. Hide treats around the cage or in one of the toys of your bird. Playing with an Indian Ringneck is all about creativity. The more you think, the more ideas you are likely to come up with. The only basics that you need to know is that the parrot loves to shred, chew, forage and pull. A toy that allows them to do one or more of the above will be adored.

4. Training your Indian Ringneck

A well trained bird is always a lot easier to handle and manage. If your Indian Ringneck has any behavioral issues, they can be sorted with training gradually. But, you need to understand that this takes a lot of patience and can be quite demanding in terms of the time you spend. Here are a few tips that you should keep in mind before you start training your Indian Ringneck:

- Establish a routine. Practice your training session at a particular time every day.

- Be patient. Do not show your bird that you are irritated or annoyed with him for not pulling off a trick. This is not natural for him and he is bound to take some time.

- Be consistent. Do not change the cues that you give the bird. If you are saying "Up" sometimes and "Come" the other time, the bird may not take the cue.

- Be abundant in your praises. Let your bird know how much you appreciate his efforts.

These tips are very important when you are training any animal. With highly intelligent creatures like Indian Ringnecks, it is a lot more challenging but is great fun too.

Target Training

Target training gives your bird something to look forward to while performing the tasks that you want him to. Target training is the best way to get your bird to do the most basic thing- getting in and out of the cage.

Give your Indian Ringneck a target that he can follow. This is most likely a treat at the end of a stick. Hold it out to the bird and allow him to take the treat. If your bird does not respond to the target initially, you can gently touch his beak with it and see how he reacts. If it is treat that your bird likes, he will go for it immediately.

Then, gradually increase the distance between your bird and the target and watch him walk up to it and take a nibble. You can then move the target around the cage and see if he follows it.

The next step is to get the bird to follow this target even when the treat is absent. He may do this the first time you present the target without the treat. If the bird does not respond to the target without the treat, then you will have to continue with the treat for a while until he forms the association between the target and the chance of getting a treat with a target.

When your bird is following the target successfully, the next step is to get him in and out of the cage. Open the cage door and hold the target at the door. He will come to take a nibble. Keep pulling it away till the bird is finally out of the cage.

Let the bird explore the area. Make sure it is free from any danger for the bird. If your Indian Ringneck has the slightest negative experience with the first time in open space, he will take a long time to regain trust.

Then, when you are ready to take the bird back into the cage, allow him to follow the target. Finish off with a treat or a toy in the cage so that he associates the cage with only positive experiences.

Step up training

Stepping up is one of the most important things you will teach your Indian Ringneck. The Indian Ringneck is a rather large bird. So, having him step up on a finger can be a little hard. The bird will step up but you may find him too heavy to handle.

The best option is to offer your forearm as the step for a bird like the Indian Ringneck. So, hold the forearm horizontally in front of the bird and place the target just behind your forearm. Then say the cue word, "Up". The bird will go for the target and will step on your forearm to reach out to it.

If the bird does not step up with the target, you can even hold his favorite treat in the similar fashion. Now, you need you keep your hand very still. The bird may nibble at your forearm. However, you must not flinch or move. An unsteady perch is one thing that all birds dislike. He is biting to make sure that this perch will not break. Chew on your lower lip and hold still.

If the bird steps up, praise him and give him a treat. Repeat this a couple of times and then try to just place your forearm before the bird and say "Up". If he climbs up without the target, you have successfully completed your step up training.

Remember that the bird has an additional incentive for stepping up- being with you. They are most likely going to learn this trick faster than any other trick because of this.

Step up training can then be extended to your shoulder or your head. That way your bird can be with you at all times as soon as you are home from work.

Step up training is also valuable in keeping your bird safe. If you are having an introduction session between your bird and other household pets, there could be some signs of aggression. If you notice this, you can get the bird to step up on your hand and take him out of a potentially dangerous situation. Even when you are escaping a natural calamity or say a fire, you can save your bird easily if he can step up faster.

Training the bird to talk

It is a lot of fun to get parrots to talk. You will be surprised at the number of words they will pick up even without you trying. By simply hearing the same word over and over again, these birds will learn them. However, you can optimize the talking ability of your bird with a few simple tricks:

- Make visual associations with the words that you want to teach them. For example, if you want to teach the bird the names of foods, say the name out in a loud pitched voice when you offer it to the bird. These birds will actually learn to differentiate between different foods. If they hear you say the name of a food they dislike, you will actually see them backing away. If you want them to say hello or bye, say the word every time you enter the room or leave the room. These visual associations helps the bird even understand the meaning of the word to some extent.

- Say the words that you want them to learn in a high pitch. They will pick up on the words that you say loudly and clearly. This even happens when you are not training the bird. So, if you have the habit of swearing loudly when you are upset, your bird may pick up on it. Just like you would avoid foul language around a baby, avoid it around your parrot too.

- There is no particular time of the day to teach the parrot to talk. It should be as repetitive as you can make it. Like a baby, a parrot needs to keep hearing you talk to pick up on words. So talk to the bird as often as you can. Another way to help the parrot learn is to keep cartoon shows on for a few hours a day. The loud pitched, high energy communication will appeal to the bird.

- When the bird says a certain word, be abundant in your praises and shower him with treats. He will repeat this behavior more often. When he associates the visual cue with the word, be prepared to be welcomed home with a loud, high pitched, "Hello!"

When your Indian Ringneck is learning new words, you will often see that he is chattering to himself. This is quite adorable to watch. This behavior is mostly a practice session of sorts for the bird to learn what he wants to say. If you have a pair of birds, you will be surprised at how much they actually learn from one another.

5. Overcoming Ringneck behavior issues

There are two common issues that all parrot owners face- aggression and screaming. These issues can be overcome with some simple training methods.

Getting the Indian Ringneck to stop biting

Biting means two things- the bird does not trust you yet, or the bird is seeking attention. If it is the former case, the biting habit will reduce eventually. However, if your bird is nippy on a frequent basis, the only thing he wants is attention.

The common thing that we all do when we are bitten is draw our hand away and scream. This is just the response that he is looking for. So, even if it really hurts, make no sound. If the bird is perched on your hand or shoulder when he bites, the "earthquake" technique is a good idea. Just wobble the perch a little immediately after he bites. This could be your shoulder or your hand.

Birds absolutely dislike an unsteady perch. They will soon associate bad behavior with an unsteady perch and stop biting. Another method that you could try is the "head down" method. All you need to do is push his head down with your index finger and softly say "No."

Make sure that your push is gentle as the bird's head is very delicate. This pressing down is very uncomfortable for your bird and he will not appreciate it. So, just to avoid getting into this position of discomfort, he will stop biting. The previous method is considered safer and more effective. It can be used to stop any undesirable behavior exhibited by your parrot including destructive behavior such as chewing. Yes, it is possible that your parrot will try to chew on your collar or earring when he is perched on the shoulder.

Getting the Indian Ringneck to stop screaming

Indian Ringneck's are usually quiet in comparison to other parrots. However, they will have bouts of screaming in the day. This is either early in the morning or sometime during the day. This is common for all birds and is not really a cause for concern. They may also scream when they are upset or startled. Screaming is considered bad behavior only when your bird screams every time you put him back in the cage or when you leave the room.

This shows separation anxiety that is not a good thing for birds. The first thing you need to do is make your bird independent. That will happen only when you establish a routine. Set your playtime with the bird. This could be a few hours in the morning and a few hours in the evening. For the rest of the time, give the bird foraging toys or other toys that will keep him busy. The bird needs to be active and playful even when you are not around. One interesting distraction for a bird is cartoon shows. They love the sounds and the visuals. You will see that their attention is maximized by certain shows. These are the favorites that he has picked. You can keep the show running and get on with your work.

If the bird still screams when you step out, do not come running back in and ask him to stop or calm down. He got the two things that he was screaming for- you and your voice. Just stay out of the room and let him shout and rant. At some point he will get quiet. Come into the room when he does that. He will then realize that you will come back to him only when he is quiet.

Then, put some foraging toys into the cage every time you leave. Then he will associate you going away with something fun to do in the cage. That will reduce the screams. He will learn to be entertained even when you are not around. To ease a screaming parrot, you need to make sure that you are giving him a lot of attention. Fix a routine and stick to it. Your parrot must feel loved and must feel like an important part of the flock.

6. Training tips for Indian Ringnecks

Here are some training tips that you need to keep in mind:

- Set a routine and stick to it if you want the training to be effective

- Use visual cues along with the clicker. This could be simple hand gestures that the bird understands.

- Training should be done in neutral ground, preferably outside the cage on a training perch that you can purchase in a store.

- Be very generous with your praise and appreciation.

- Punishment does not go down well with parrots. They will stop responding.

- Never mix up cues. That will confuse your bird.

- When you are using verbal cues, be very assertive and clear in what you are saying.

Once you have formed a good bond with your bird, you can be certain that you will have a wonderful companion for the rest of your life. They will love you unconditionally and will do the best they can to please you and make you happy.

Chapter 7: Breeding Indian Ringnecks

If you plan to breed your Indian Ringneck, the first thing to do is to check the breeding laws as mentioned before. If your state allows breeding of Ringnecks, you need wait till they are 2-3 years old. That is when the bird is fully sexually mature.

Making sure that you find a suitable partner and provide conditions that are ideal for your bird to breed in are essential. This includes providing a conducive environment and also ensuring that the brooding female gets the nutrition she requires to raise a healthy clutch.

1. Introducing a mate

The best thing to do would be to decide if you want to breed your bird or not right in the beginning. That way you can bring home a male and a female and raise them together to be mates. The good thing about Indian Ringnecks is that they remain close to their human friends despite forming very strong bonds with the partner. Also, if you change your mind later about rearing fledglings, you can always prevent breeding by not providing the ideal conditions for the birds. If you have a male or female bird and you want to find a suitable partner, it may require a good amount of patience.

When you decide to introduce older birds to each other, the first thing to do is quarantining the new bird. Then, you must keep in mind that the female will be more aggressive and territorial than the male. These birds will dictate the whole relationship, the breeding season and also the rearing of the offspring. So, if you have a female Indian Ringneck, the introduction must happen in a new and neutral environment where the female is less likely to be territorial. Follow the same steps mentioned in the earlier chapters about the introduction of two birds.

The next thing to do is to check whether the birds are showing any bonding behavior. The first sign is that the birds are feeding each other. If you do not see this behavior, you can give them wood that they can chew. This is a part of the courtship ritual and you will eventually see them starting to feed one another. Only when you see this consistently should you provide a nesting box. Never provide a nesting box before the birds have bonded.

This will make the female hide in the nesting box all day and your birds will most likely not mate. Even if the birds do mate, the eggs that are laid are clear. They will not produce any chicks when they hatch.

Once the nesting box has been introduced after the birds have bonded, the male will initiate mating. During this phase you need to give the birds a larger portion of food. This will allow them to believe that they can provide for their young when they are born. Avoid touching the birds during this time. Also, avoid loud music or any other stressful conditions for the birds.

In the first few days of introduction, you need to watch the birds extremely carefully. If you see that one of them is excessively aggressive towards the other, they may not be a compatible pair. Simply separate the birds. In case you are providing the bird with any supplements, be very cautious. If one of them is getting an overdose of the supplement, he or she may become aggressive and hyperactive leading you to believe that the birds are not compatible while they may actually be the perfect pair.

2. Preparing for the breeding season

Birds require very specific conditions in order to breed. They are shy creatures and will not breed if there is too much disturbance. You need to first shift the cage of the birds to a room in the house that is quiet, but has a good supply of natural light. You can lay a cloth over the cage for the birds to escape into when they want to rest.

Unless there is a proper nesting place available for the birds, they are very unlikely to mate. Keeping a nesting box just outside the cage will encourage them to mate. The box should be fixed at a height from the floor of the cage. It can be placed on the play area of you have a play top cage.

Instead of using cardboard boxes, it best to get a store made nesting box for your Indian Ringneck. These nesting boxes made of wood or metal are not destroyed easily. They can be used for all the breeding seasons making the birds feel comfortable. These boxes are also easier to clean. You need to remember that Indian Ringneck chicks can be very messy.

Choose a vertical nesting box that measures at least 18X18X36 inches. These boxes usually have an entrance door and a separate inspection door that you can access.

The nesting box should be placed in such a way that the birds have a good view of the room around them. The cage should have a solid perch for the birds. Place one inside the cage and one outside leading to the nest box. This allows them to access the nest. These perches should be made of hardwood as the females are likely to chew on them when they become hormonal.

Leaving a few soft wood options is a good idea to help the bird chew it and release some stress. With this arrangement, your birds will get ready to mate. The male will mount the female a couple of times. In two weeks the female will lay her first clutch of eggs. The eggs of the Ringneck parrot are the size of a quarter and are laid every alternate day until the clutch is complete. The number of eggs in a clutch can vary from 3 to 6 eggs. The eggs are white in color.

Diet for the breeding season

You need to make sure that the birds have adequate nutrients to produce the necessary hormones and have a successful breeding season. For the females, especially, the diet is of utmost importance.

Adding assorted nuts to the diet will help the bird to a large extent. Each nut has specific functions that aid the breeding season. Here are a few nuts that you should include and the benefits of these nuts:

- Macadamia nuts- They provide the additional fats that are required in a bird's diet during this season.
- Walnuts- They provide the birds with necessary omega 3 fatty acids.
- Filberts- They are a great source of calcium for the females.
- Pistachios- They aid vitamin A in large amounts.

In addition to that you can also provide coconut, eggs and fresh fruits and vegetables. The nutrition of the bird determines the final quality of the eggs that are produced during this season.

You can even provide fortified pellets or supplements under the guidance of your vet to give your birds the additional nutrition boost that they require.

3. Artificial incubation of the eggs

Sometimes, Indian Ringnecks may abandon their clutch after a few days. This is when you need to intervene and take care of the eggs yourself. Sometimes you will also notice that the hen also destroys a couple of the eggs.

To incubate the eggs, you can purchase a standard incubator from any pet supply store. You can also order them online. It is never advisable to prepare your own incubator as the temperature settings need to be very accurate to hatch the eggs successfully. The incubation period will be the same as the natural incubation period.

The incubator is a one-time investment that is completely worth it if you choose to breed more Indian Ringnecks even in the next season.

Here are a few tips to incubate the eggs correctly:

- Pick the eggs up with clean hands. The chicks are extremely vulnerable to diseases and can be affected even with the smallest traces of microbes. Only pick eggs that are visibly clean. If there is a lot of debris or poop on a certain egg, it is best not to mix it with the other eggs as it will cause unwanted infections.

- Wash the eggs gently to clean the surface. The next step is to candle the eggs. This means you will have to hold the egg up to a light. If you can see the embryo in the form of a dark patch, it means that the egg is fertile. On the other hand, if all you can see is an empty space inside the egg, it is probably not going to hatch.

- In the natural setting, the eggs are usually given heat on one side while the other side remains cooler. Then the hen may turn the eggs with her movements. It is impossible to heat the egg evenly even if you have a fan type incubator that heats up the interior of the egg quite evenly.

- The next thing to keep in mind is the transfer from the nest box to the incubator. Line a container with wood shavings and place the eggs away from each other. Even the slightest bump can crack an egg. You need to know that a cracked egg has very few chances of hatching.

- The incubator will also have a humidifier that will maintain the moisture levels inside the incubator. The temperature and the humidity should be set as per the readings advised for Indian Ringnecks. That is the ideal condition for the eggs to hatch.

- In case you want to be doubly sure, you can also check the temperature with a mercury thermometer regularly.

- It is safest to place the eggs on the side when you put them in the incubator. They are stable and will not have any damage or accident.

- Heating the eggs evenly is the most important thing when it comes to the chances of hatching the egg. Make sure you turn the eggs every two hours over 16 hours. This should be done an odd number of times. The next step is to turn the eggs by 180 degrees once every day.

- Keep a close watch on the eggs in the incubator. It is best that you get an incubator with a see-through lid. This will let you observe and monitor the eggs. If you notice that one of them has cracked way before the incubation period ends, take it out of the incubator. If the eggs have a foul smelling discharge, begin to take an abnormal shape or change color, you need to remove them as they could be carrying diseases that will destroy the whole clutch.

- Usually, Indian Ringneck eggs will pip after 24-48 hours of the completion of the incubation period.

- The hatching of the egg begins when the carbon dioxide levels in the egg increase. This starts the hatching process. All baby birds have an egg tooth which allows them to tear the inner membrane open. Then they continue to tear the egg shell to come out.

- The muscles of the chick twitch in order to strengthen them and to make sure that he is able to tear the egg shell out successfully.

- Never try to assist the hatching process unless you are a professional. If you feel like your chicks are unable to break out of the egg shell, you can call your vet immediately.

Watching the eggs hatch is a magical experience. You can do a few small things to make your clutch more successful. For instance, if you are buying a brand new incubator, turn on the recommended settings and keep it on for at least two weeks before you expect the eggs to be placed in them.

Make sure that the incubator is not disturbed. Keep all the wires tucked in to prevent someone from tripping on it and disturbing the set up or turning the incubator off. It is best to place this incubator in areas like the basement that are seldom used by you or your family members.

4. Raising the chicks

Towards the end of the incubation period, you need to set up a brooding box which can either be purchased or even created using a simple cardboard box. This is where the chicks will be raised until they are large enough to feed on their own and occupy a cage.

Now, this box needs to have an internal temperature of 36degrees centigrade. You can maintain this using a heating lamp. If you do not feel confident to do this, you can just buy a readymade brooder. These brooders have recommended settings that will ensure that your bird is in safe hands.

As soon as the egg hatches, the hatchlings should be shifted to this brooder or brooding box.

Young birds are seldom able to feed on their own. You will have to make sure that you give the birds the nutrition that they need by hand-feeding them.

Your vet will be able to recommend a good baby bird formula that you can feed the hatchlings. All you have to do is mix the formula as per the instructions on the box. Then using a clean syringe or ink dropper, you can feed the babies.

When you are feeding the bird, make sure that you place him on a towel because this is going to be a rather messy task. Then hold the head of the bird between two fingers and push the upper jaw gently. The bird will open his mouth automatically. Then, you will have to hold the syringe to the left of the bird's mouth or to your right and then let the food in. This ensures that your bird does not choke on the food that you are giving him.

When the birds are done eating, they will automatically refuse the feed. You will have to feed hatchlings at least once every two hours. Make sure that you watch the body language of the bird. If he is resisting the feed, you can wait a little longer and then do the same.

As the birds grow the number of feeding sessions will reduce. Ideally, by the time the feathers of the birds appear, they will be feeding about three times every day.

The next step is to wean the birds or make them independent eaters. This can be done when the birds are about 7 weeks old. You can introduce solid foods like pellets and fruits to the bird along with the handfed formula.

Just place a few pieces of fruit or some pellets in front of the bird and wait for him to taste it. If he likes it, he may eat a little and then move on to the formula. Try introducing different fruits and vegetables and notice which ones are tempting enough for the bird to leave the formula for.

You can replace one meal with the favorite food of the bird and add a few pellets too. You will notice that eventually the birds will eat when they are hungry and will not accept the hand fed formula. That is when they are fully weaned.

Incubating the egg artificially has several advantages. To begin with, it encourages the parent birds to lay another clutch of eggs. Next, it increases the chances of the egg hatching. As for hand feeding, it makes your birds familiar with people and will also make them easier to train. Indian Ringnecks are known to be bad at parenting and are notorious for leaving their babies hungry.

On the other hand, when a bird is raised by the parents, they will develop a parenting instinct that is better than that of a hand fed bird. They are likely to be better breeders.

The best thing to do would be to allow the birds to feed the little ones for a while. Then you can intervene and help the babies wean. This is called mixed parenting and is best for those who intend to breed Indian Ringnecks commercially.

Chapter 8: When Life Changes

With all the planning, you can never predict the course that your life will take. What if you have to make some important decisions that may affect your journey with your parrot? After all, this is a commitment of 30-50 years. No one can plan that far ahead practically.

However, you can deal with life changes and still have your parrot with you. Here are some things that you need to know when you become a parent to an Indian Ringneck.

1. Moving homes

This is one of the most common challenges faced by parrot owners. It is likely that you will move at least once in the time that you have with your parrot. If you are moving locally, it is easier. However, when you have to travel overseas, there are various permits involved in the process. We will talk about both these situations in these sections.

Moving in your city

If you are moving to another part of your city, make sure you drive up. Do not opt for any other form of transport as it may stress your bird out. The first thing to do would be to get your bird used to travelling by a car.

You need to train your bird to like the car as soon as possible. After all, your vet visits are going to be by car in all likeness. To begin with, just get the bird used to the interiors of the car. Get a separate travel cage. This allows the bird to understand that when he is transferred to this cage, he is going out on a drive.

Make sure the interiors of the car are set to room temperature. Place the cage inside the car and let it stay there for a few minutes. Stay in the car with the bird and see how he reacts. If he settles in one corner of the cage or starts bobbing his tail, it means that he is upset. If this aggravates, just take him back home and let him rest.

Do this a couple of times till you know that the bird is comfortable in the car. Then, take short drives around the block. During these drives talk to the bird in a calming voice. After a while, they will start enjoying the drive as it gives them more time with you.

As moving day approaches, start loading the car up with all your bags and taking short drives. If your bird needs to travel a long distance with these bags all of a sudden, he will be upset. Let him get used to the different shapes and sizes.

When the final day comes, take the drive easy. Take a break every time and let the bird relax. Make sure enough food and water is available. The substrate should have a few more layers so that the cage stays clean. After you reach home, find a good room to place the cage in. Then, you will have to follow the same housebreaking process mentioned earlier in this book.

Moving to a different state or country

Indian Ringnecks are allowed in most states and countries. However, you may have to take appropriate permits to ensure that your bird clears customs without any stress. Your vet or your breeder should be able to help you with this. The laws have been laid out to ensure that there is no illegal trade of birds. The three most important laws are the Wildlife Conservation Act, Convention of the International Trade in Endangered Species of Wild Fauna and Flora and the Endangered Species Act.

The websites of these laws will tell you how you may obtain permits, if your bird needs one. Usually, it takes up to 60 seconds to get a permit. It only requires a simple application that you need to fill up and submit.

The stressful part in travelling overseas is getting your bird on a plane. Make sure you survey all the airlines to pick the most pet friendly one. If you need to take connecting flights, make sure that you take the same airlines to keep the regulations and rules consistent.

The airlines usually have guidelines with respect to the carrier you will use for travel. You will also need to get a health certificate from your vet which will certify that your bird is healthy enough to travel. Some airlines make it mandatory to have these certificates attested by the USDA or the Animal and Plant Inspection Service. This certificate should not be more than 10 days old.

It is a good idea to have the wings clipped. This will make it easier for the bird to be handled when he is crossing customs. A bird harness is a good idea to ensure that your bird is not tossed around during the trip.

Now, you need to understand that the bird will be placed in the cargo area. That means he will be stressed out. You need to make sure that the cage is 100% comfortable to reduce any stress. Place enough food and fresh water in the cage. Even mix in a few of your bird's favorite treats. You also need to make sure that the quantity is appropriate for the travel time. Adding a few toys will also keep the bird busy during this transit. You must lay a well absorbing substrate on the base of the cage. This will keep the cage clean. If your flight is really long, you need to check if the airline makes any arrangements for feeding and changing water. This service will be available at an extra cost.

When the trip is over, you are likely to have a very stressed bird to take care of. The first thing to do would be to get him to a vet and have him checked. Then, leave him on a quiet room in the new house and keep talking to him in a soft and comforting voice.

2. Getting a demanding job

When you brought home your Indian Ringneck, you may have had a very relaxed job. Of course, you are likely to make progress in the two decades that your bird will spend with you. Then, your job may become demanding, requiring you to spend long hours at the office or travel frequently. That is when you need to make appropriate arrangements for your bird to be taken care of. You need to find someone trustworthy to be with your bird while you are away.

The first and the best option is to ask a friend or relative who has some experience with birds. They should know how to handle the bird, manage emergencies and even keep the bird entertained. Of course, they should be committed towards taking care of your bird. It is best that they stay in your home and care for the bird to reduce the stress of shifting. However, if no one is available to fill in for you in your absence, there are a few more options you can try.

Your avian vet will probably be associated with a pet hostel or may have one of his own. If you get any references, you can check the facility out to make sure that it is a safe and clean environment for your bird. You need to be additionally cautious with birds as they are extremely susceptible to infections.

The other option available is to find a good pet sitter for your bird. This can be a tedious process requiring you to conduct several interviews and find someone who is experienced with Indian Ringnecks. Always hire a sitter from a professional agency to ensure accountability. You can check with the National Association of Professional Pet Sitters or The Pet Sitters International to help you find a good sitter for your bird. Here are some simple things that will tell you that your sitter is good for your bird:

- He or she has some experience with Indian Ringneck parrots in particular.
- They have commercial liability insurance which tells you that they are solely responsible should anything go wrong with your bird.
- They will give you an official contract that states all the costs and the services provided in complete detail. NEVER make verbal agreements with a sitter.
- The sitter is comfortable while handling your bird and seems experienced with birds of various behavior patterns.
- The contract must state all the arrangements that will be made if your bird falls sick or needs emergency care.
- Also, if your pet sitter is unable to attend to your bird, they should have a substitute ready.

When you decide to hire a particular sitter, make sure that he or she spends some time with your bird before you leave the two alone. Hand over all the details like your bird's diet, medications and the number of the vet in writing. This ensures proper care for the bird while you are away.

3. Having a baby

Although it seems like your parrot will not be affected by the new baby in your home, the truth is that you have to put in a lot of effort to keep the parrot happy. Just like you had to prepare yourself for the arrival of your bird, your bird also needs to be prepared for the arrival of the baby.

For a month prior to the delivery of the baby, you need to start dabbing yourself with baby powder to get the bird accustomed to the scents. Then, you must also change and cuddle with a swaddle doll in the presence of your bird. Some owners say that playing CDs of baby cooing sounds also helped the bird get used to the new baby when it arrived. You can even find these sounds online.

Parrots mix well with babies. However, there is an element of jealousy if you do not make the parrot feel emotionally secure. Then, the parrot may become aggressive and nippy towards the child. This is when most people will have to give their beloved parrot up to make their home safe for their new born child.

You will never have to get there if you take a few simple measures beforehand. Indian Ringnecks, by nature, are very kind and friendly birds. These birds take their flock very seriously. In this case, you are your bird's flock. If you make your parrot feel left out when the baby arrives, he will begin to feel like he is being shunned out of the flock.

The first rule is to make sure that you talk to your parrot and play with him when the baby is in the room. You must not let the bird out of the cage until the baby is older. However, your parrot needs to know that you are giving him attention even when the baby is around. If you only attend to your bird when the baby is sleeping, he will learn that he gets to spend time with you only when the baby is away. That makes him jealous and, in some cases, aggressive. They may also resort to habits like feather plucking.

Before the baby comes home, you need to make sure that your parrot is independent. He should be able to keep himself engaged even when you are a little busy. Socializing the bird is very important in this case. He should see you interact with many people and should be accustomed to sharing your love with other human beings. Only when you have developed a strong bond with your bird should you think about having a baby. Yes, your parrot is a very important part of your decision to have a child.

Indian Ringneck tip: If you have just had a baby, do not bring a new bird home. It is not just overwhelming for you to take care of two babies, but may also make the bird feel neglected, leading to unwanted behavioral issues.

Chapter 9: The Health of the Indian Ringneck

When fed well and kept active, Indian Ringnecks rarely fall sick. These birds are not as susceptible to health issues as the other birds of this family. Usually, poor sanitation and diet can lead to health issues in Indian Ringnecks. This chapter discusses the most common health problems observed in Indian Ringnecks and gives you a great deal of information about keeping your Indian Ringneck healthy and free from these common health problems.

a. Signs of illnesses

Birds show very obvious changes in their demeanor when they are unwell. You will also notice very obvious physical signs that can tell you, without any doubt that your bird is suffering from some disease or infection.

If you see any of the following signs in your Indian Ringneck, see a vet immediately. Do not wait and see if these symptoms subside. That is a common mistake made by most bird owners.

The signs to look out for:

- The bird is crouching close to the perch and fluffing the feathers up as though he is trying to gather up a lot of warmth.
- Regurgitation that is not related to breeding behavior.
- Sudden weakness
- Refusal to eat food
- Abnormal sneezing. Birds do sneeze for several reasons such as dust, irritants, sudden change in weather, their own feathers getting into their nose etc. However, if the bird sneezes without a break, it is a problem.
- There is dry mucus around the nares or the nasal passage.
- The bird does not poop as much. While this may seem like a good thing to you, it is actually a sign of depleting health as far as the bird is concerned.
- Sudden aggression or lack of interest.
- Unusual colored droppings. Some foods may also cause a change in coloration. However, you need to consult a vet.

- Feather plucking.
- Biting or nipping unusually.
- Diarrhea
- A marked reduction in vocalization.
- Deposits or dried up feces around the cloaca.
- Vomiting. The difference between vomiting and regurgitation is the bird's behavior. If your bird shakes his head while getting the food out, he is vomiting.
- Incessant tail bobbing
- Inability to walk properly, stand, perch or fly.
- Seizures
- Abnormal tilting of the head. If the head tilts and seems like the bird has no control over it, you are definitely looking at a bird that is extremely unwell.

There are some infections and diseases that commonly affect parrots. Some of them can be fatal. However, most of them can be detected early and given the appropriate treatment to prevent any casualty. The more time you spend with your bird, the more aware you will become of his normal behavior. So, even the slightest change in this will help you get your bird appropriate care in time. The next section talks about these diseases and symptoms in detail.

b. Common health issues

Aspergillosis

This condition is also called Mycotic pneumonia or brooder pneumonia. It affects the lungs of your Indian Ringneck. This is a disease that is common in birds that are kept in unclean cages. The damp areas of the cage become breeding grounds for the aspegilla fungus which is responsible for the infection.

The common signs of this condition are lethargy, depression, mucus formation in the nares and strained breathing. These signs are due to the congested air sacs. In some cases the virus may affect the nervous system, leading to paralysis. In the later and more acute stages anorexia and dysponea is seen in the birds. Sometimes, it can even lead to sudden death.

Good sanitation is the first step towards preventing this condition. When your bird is already infected, the common medication prescribed includes fluconazole and intraconazole.

Sarcocystosis

This condition is common in any Psittacine birds that have originated in Australia, Asia or Africa. Caused by a protozoan called Sarcocystis falcatula, this disease was introduced in these birds by opossums. This condition is not contagious among birds. However, if you have multiple birds at home you will notice that most of them will get affected at the same time as the virus is left on the floor of the cage.

The first step towards prevention is keeping the cage away from predators of any sort. Next, regular cleaning of the cage will prevent the infection to a large extent.

Now, this condition is hyperacute. This means that it does not have any symptoms and can be fatal to the bird. That is why this condition is very difficult to diagnose. When the dead bird is lifted, you will see a clear fluid flowing out of its mouth.

In very rare cases, the bird will how signs like labored breathing, yellow colored droppings and extreme lethargy. That is when a lung biopsy is done to confirm the condition.

Sadly, no documented treatment is available for the condition. One of the only medicines that have been administered for birds with this condition is Pyrimethamine. Even this is not a guaranteed cure for the condition.

Beak and Feather Disease

Also known as Psittacine Beak and Feather Disease of PBFD, this is one of the most lethal conditions in birds that belong to this family. Caused by unsanitary conditions, this disease has no recorded cure. If your bird is diagnosed with this condition, it is usually euthanized to prevent further deterioration or possible infection in other birds.

Although Indian Ringnecks do not have as much feather dust as other psittacines, they are just as susceptible to the condition. Usually, these birds get the disease from dried droppings. You will notice an abnormality in the development of new feathers after the molting season. The beak will begin to look dull. In chicks, the development of the beak is very abnormal. This is a progressive condition that will lead to paralysis or death in the bird. It can only be prevented with proper sanitation.

Liver Problems

This is a common condition in Indian Ringnecks. Their long digestive tract tends to absorb more and retain the excess calories as fat. Liver diseases occur in these parrots when the tissue of the liver will slowly be replaced by fat. Although the condition is slow, the symptoms appear all of a sudden.

This condition occurs in females more commonly. It is also seen in juvenile birds. Any excessive calories in a bird will be converted to calories and stored in the bird. That is why you need to make sure that you maintain a well-balanced diet for the bird.

The common symptom is change in the color of the feathers in an adult bird. Only when it occurs upon birth is change in color considered mutation. Other problems include stressed breathing due to an enlargement in the liver, distended abdomen, diarrhea, unusual droppings, itchy skin, softness around the beak of the bird and even inability to clot blood. This means even an accidentally broken blood feather can be fatal for the bird.

You need to put your bird in a quiet environment so the he can get a lot of sleep. Restorative sleep is needed. In addition to that, you will have to provide the bird with the diet prescribed by the vet. This is usually a fiber rich diet.

Toe Tapping

Toe tapping is not a health issue, per say. It is more a symptom that is indicative of multiple health issues in an Indian Ringneck. First, it is an indication of some form of severe infection in the bird. In some cases, when the hen is hormonal, she will indicate it by tapping her toe vigorously. Last, and most common, is insufficient nutrition or improper nutrition. Whether the nutrients are excessive or under the recommended amount, toe tapping occurs.

This is noticed mostly at night when the bird is asleep. You will hear continuous tapping on the perch. This condition requires immediate attention. You can prevent it by keeping the bird in a hygienic environment and by providing him with the necessary diet.

Polyoma

This is an infection caused by the Polyoma virus. It is usually seen in baby birds at about 7 weeks of age. They will have sudden bruises on the skin along with symptoms like a swollen belly, weakness, wobbly feet and abnormal development of the feathers. In some cases, regurgitation and diarrhea is also observed. There may be some symptoms that resemble liver disease.

A vaccination is available for this condition. Polyoma vaccination must be given to the chicks when they are about 40 days old. After two weeks you can give them a booster shots. This keeps them safe usually. However, it is a good idea to get booster shots every year for your bird. If you have breeding birds, they need to be vaccinated at least two times before the breeding season begins.

Gout

This is another condition that commonly affects the chicks. In case of any calcification in the kidneys, the birds develop gout. You may observe these symptoms in the bird when he is between 4 and 8 weeks old if the level of calcium in the food is improper.

The earliest symptoms include vomiting and slight dehydration. This may also be a sign of a bacterial infection. However, get a blood test done immediately. If left unattended, the bird will not be able to retain anything that he consumes. You will also notice that the skin on the chest shrinks.

You must always have enough clean drinking water available for your birds. Allopurinal and Colchicine are the recommended medicines for this condition.

As you can see in all the conditions mentioned above, diet and poor sanitation are the primary contributors to any health problems in your bird. So, be very careful in these two aspects and you can prevent most diseases. A large part of your bird's health depends on the preventive are that you provide. The following sections tell you everything that you need to know about preventive care.

c. Dealing with injuries and accidents

Besides infections and congenital conditions, a lot of bird owners need to deal with several accidents that may cause injuries or other problems for your bird. Here are three of the most common problems that you are likely to face with your Indian Ringneck:

Broken blood feathers

When a blood feather breaks, it will bleed profusely. You need to make sure that you pack the shaft with flour or styptic powder. You will get a styptic pencil in your local supermarket. You must cover this with gauze and press it gently. Then take your bird to the vet to have the shaft removed. With experience, you will learn to remove this shaft yourself.

Animal attack

If you have a cat or a dog at home and your bird has been attacked, you need to make sure that your bird gets first aid immediately. The first thing that you will do is calm to bird down, if the bird is not seriously injured. Shift him to a calm and quiet place and let him settle down. Then, examine the wounds.

Any bleeding should be stopped using gauze. DO NOT use the styptic pencil in this case. If you notice that the wing is broken, hold it close to the body and tie it loosely using the gauze. Then, rush your pet to the vet immediately. Remember, the mouth of a cat or dog carries several bacteria that can be toxic for a bird. So, every wound needs to be examined immediately.

Burns

In case your bird has an accidental burn by sitting on a hot stove or brushing against a hot container, you need to run cold water on the area that is affected for a while. Then, dab the area dry using a clean gauze. A cold compress can be applied to the area to provide immediate relief. A severe burn needs immediate veterinary care as the bird may be very stressed. You may have to provide certain antibiotics to ensure that there is no infection.

Poisoning

Poisoning can occur for several reasons. The bird may inhale the toxic fumes from a Teflon pan, ingest something poisonous or even come in contact with metals like lead and zinc. You will notice that your bird's beak is wide open, along with labored breathing and rapid wagging of the tail. If the bird has inhaled or ingested the toxin, call your vet immediately. Alternatively, you can call the **ASPCA National Animal Poison Control Center** on 888-4ANI-HELP (888-426-4435). They will want exact details about the type of toxin involved, the weight of your bird, when the exposure occurred and the symptoms that your bird is showing.

If you see that his eyes have been affected by the toxin, the eyes need to be washed before you take the bird to a vet.

d. First aid kit

You can never be sure when a bird needs emergency care. With Indian Ringnecks, they are so active and playful that a few accidents are bound to occur. You need to make sure that you are prepared at all times to handle these emergencies. For starters, you need a fully equipped first aid kit that is available always. The kit must contain:

- All the contact details and the necessary directions to your vet's clinic.
- Emergency and trauma clinic number in case your vet does not take emergency cases or is unavailable.
- Number of the poison control centre.
- Clean and sterile gauze.
- Q-tips to apply any ointment or to clean up the wound.
- Scissors to remove any string that has caused a cut or injury of to cut the bandage.
- Tape for broken wings
- Gauze roll for broken wings.
- Recommended antibiotic ointment.
- Hydrogen peroxide or betadine to clean any wound.

- Styptic powder or pencil to clot blood.
- A gram scale to check the bird's weight.
- Heating pad in case your bird suffers from sudden chills or cold
- Towels to handle and restrain the bird when needed
- Thermometer
- Syringe or a medicine dropper

With this, you are more or less prepared to handle any emergency related to your bird. If you are unsure about any injury or symptom, always call your vet.

e. Preventive care

Prevention is better than cure, especially in the case of delicate and vulnerable creatures like birds. If you want your Indian Ringneck to always stay healthy, you need to take the following preventive care measures:

- The bird must be groomed and kept clean.
- Keep the bird active physically and mentally.
- Always quarantine any new bird that you bring to your home.
- Make sure that your home is parrot proofed before you let the bird out of the cage.
- The bird should get ample sunlight.
- Regular visits to the vet are a must. Never miss an annual check up.
- Clean drinking water should be available for the bird at all times.
- The cage and the toys must be cleaned regularly.

An Indian Ringneck also needs lots of love to stay healthy. Make sure that your bird is getting a lot of attention from you. And, with the above mentioned measures, you are sure to raise happy and healthy birds.

Is Insurance necessary?

It is not easy to find insurance for pet birds. You see, these creatures are so delicate and susceptible to infections and injuries that most insurance companies do not provide proper coverage for them.

Most bird owners just put aside money in a separate account to function as insurance in case of an emergency. This is a good habit but is never reliable. There will always come a time when you may put your needs or the needs of the family first making the funds available in case of an emergency.

So, despite the fact that pet bird insurance is not perfect, it is advisable that you invest in one for some security in the future. Do some research before you actually pick insurance for your bird. Some features that your insurance plan needs to have include:

✓ Coverage for veterinary expenses. This must also include diagnosis and the actual treatment. Some of them will also pay a part of the consultation fee. These medical fees will have a limit as Indian Ringnecks have long lives. Usually, the cost covered per year is about $1500 or £3000.

✓ In case of escape or death of the bird, the market value of the bird may be reimbursed if it belongs to a rare species. For this, you should make sure that your bird has had his first health check up within 72 hours of bringing him home and also a sturdy and secure cage.

✓ Third party liability. If your bird causes any damage to another person or another person's property, the expenses incurred will be covered.

✓ Overseas travel coverage. When you travel with your bird, costs incurred upon the permits and special airline fees may be covered by some insurance companies.

The premium on an insurance plan that offers all of the above features will work up to about $150 or £300 per month. You can eliminate some features if you want to cut the costs down. When you have more than one bird, you may avail up to 10% off on each additional bird in your home.

The two most commonly chosen pet insurances for pet birds are Pet Assure and Veterinary Pet Insurance. Other pet insurances do not cover birds under them.

Chapter 10: How Expensive is an Indian Ringneck?

As we mentioned before, your Indian Ringneck is a lifelong commitment. Of course, you need to be able to fund all the needs of your parrot. This chapter will tell you exactly how much you will need in a month along with the one-time initial costs. Only if you can afford it should you bring an Indian Ringneck home.

- The cost of the bird: $150-$800 or £70-£500
- The cost of the cage: $150-400 or £80-200.
- Food per month: $80 or £35
- Toys per month: $30 or £15
- Vet costs per month: $50 or £25
- Insurance cost per month: $280 or £150

On average, you need close to $300 or £150 every month. If you think that this is manageable month after month for almost 20 years, you are ready for an Indian Ringneck.

Conclusion

Being a parent to any pet is a big responsibility. But, when you gain control of your life with your pet, it is nothing but fun and a lot of excitement. The more you work towards your bond with your Indian Ringneck, the more you will be rewarded.

These birds are delightful pets. They simply bring the whole house to life with their talking and their goofy antics. I hope that this book will be your companion through your journey with your Indian Ringneck.

If you are still thinking of bringing a bird home, this book will help you make an informed decision. Once you have brought the bird home, you will hopefully find the help that you need when some of the strangest doubts pop in your mind.

Thank you for choosing this book. And, kudos to you for making the effort to learn about the bird before bringing one home.

References

The information with respect to Indian Ringnecks available out there is never ending. It can become confusing for you to find information that is genuine and reliable. Here are a few options that you can use as reference whenever you need a little more assistance to raise your Indian Ringneck. Remember, the more you learn, the easier it will become to handle your bird.

Note: at the time of printing, all the websites below were working. As the internet changes rapidly, some sites might no longer be live when you read this book. That is, of course, out of our control.

www.indianRingneck.com

www.animalplanet85.blogspot.in

www.parrotsecrets.com

www.beautyofbirds.com

www.naturechest.com

www.birdsville.net.au

www.kijiji.ca

www.parrotsecrets.com

www.thespruce.com

www.parrotsdailynews.com

www.animals.mom.me

www.pets.thenest.com

www.sciencedirect.com

www.informationvine.com

www.peteducation.com

www.quora.com

www.parrotsnaturally.com

www.parrotscanada.com

www.adoptapet.com

www.companionparrots.org

www.linkinghub.elsevier.com

www.pets.thenest.com

www.astepupbird.com/

www.longtailedparakeets.blogspot.com

www.northernparrots.com

www.windycityparrot.com

www.pbspettravel.co.uk

www.Ringneckranch.net

www.riveroflifefarm.com